USDA

United States
Department of
Agriculture

Forest Service

Pacific Northwest
Research Station

General Technical Report
PNW-GTR-825

July 2010

Woody Biomass for Bioenergy and Biofuels in the United States— A Briefing Paper

Eric M. White

Authors

Eric M. White is a research associate, Department of Forest Engineering, Resources and Management, College of Forestry, Oregon State University, Corvallis, OR 97331.

Published with joint venture agreement between the USDA Forest Service, Pacific Northwest Research Station, Forest Products Laboratory, and Oregon State University.

Cover photo by Dave Nicholls.

Abstract

White, Eric M. 2010. Woody biomass for bioenergy and biofuels in the United States—a briefing paper. Gen. Tech. Rep. PNW-GTR-825. Portland, OR: U.S. Department of Agriculture, Forest Service, Pacific Northwest Research Station. 45 p.

Woody biomass can be used for the generation of heat, electricity, and biofuels. In many cases, the technology for converting woody biomass into energy has been established for decades, but because the price of woody biomass energy has not been competitive with traditional fossil fuels, bioenergy production from woody biomass has not been widely adopted. However, current projections of future energy use and renewable energy and climate change legislation under consideration suggest increased use of both forest and agriculture biomass energy in the coming decades. This report provides a summary of some of the existing knowledge and literature related to the production of woody biomass from bioenergy with a particular focus on the economic perspective. The most commonly discussed woody biomass feedstocks are described along with results of existing economic modeling studies related to the provision of biomass from short-rotation woody crops, harvest residues, and hazardous-fuel reduction efforts. Additionally, the existing social science literature is used to highlight some challenges to widespread production of biomass energy.

Keywords: Forest bioenergy, climate change, forest resources.

Summary

Forests are expected to have an important role in climate change mitigation under future climate change policy. Currently, much of the interest in forests centers on the opportunity to sequester carbon as part of a cap and trade policy. In addition to sequestering emitted carbon, forest resources reduce carbon emissions at the source when substituted for the fossil fuels currently used to generate heat, electricity, and transportation fuels. Woody biomass can be used to generate heat or electricity solely or in a combined heat and power (CHP) plant. As an energy feedstock, woody biomass can be used alone or in combination with other energy sources, such as coal. The technology to convert woody biomass to ethanol is established, but no commercial-scale cellulosic ethanol plants are currently in operation.

About 2 percent of the energy consumed annually in the United States is generated from wood and wood-derived fuels. Of the renewable energy consumed (including that from hydroelectric dams), 27 percent is generated from wood and wood-derived fuels. The majority of bioenergy produced from woody biomass is consumed by the industrial sector—mostly at pulp and paper mills using heat or electricity produced onsite from mill residues. U.S. Department of Energy baseline projections indicate that wood and wood-derived fuels will account for 9 percent of the energy consumed in 2030. Climate change policies that promote bioenergy production could lead to greater future woody biomass energy consumption.

The woody biomass feedstocks most likely to be supplied at low prices (e.g., $10 to $20/ton) are those that are low cost to procure, such as wood in municipal solid waste, milling residues, and some timber harvesting residues. As biomass feedstock prices increase (e.g., $25 to $40/ton), it is likely that more milling residues would become available for energy production (drawn away from existing production uses) along with more timber harvest residues. From the most recent estimates available for the United States, there are approximately 14 million dry tons of wood in municipal solid waste and construction debris, 87 million dry tons of woody milling residues, and 64 million dry tons of forest harvest residues produced annually. Biomass from short-rotation woody crops (SRWC) (and other energy crops) and agriculture residues (e.g., corn stover and husks) would likely be utilized for bioenergy at moderate feedstock prices. At the highest feedstock prices (e.g., above $50), it is likely that energy crops (e.g., SRWC) and agriculture residues will provide the greatest amounts of bioenergy feedstock. At moderate and high feedstock prices, some small-diameter material, generated either from hazard-fuel reduction or precommercial thinning could become available for bioenergy. Recent studies have estimated that about 210 million oven dry tons of small-diameter and harvest residue material could be removed through hazard-fuel treatments in the West.

There are regional disparities in the potential supplies of woody biomass. Urban wood waste availability generally follows the population distribution with some local differences related to construction and waste generation rates. Mill and harvest residues follow the regional distribution of harvesting and timber processing with most activity in the South Central and Southeast regions. The potential supply of energy crops largely mirrors the distribution of existing cropland, with significant potential plantation areas in the Corn Belt, Lake States, and South Central regions. Hazard-fuel volumes that could be used for bioenergy are located primarily in the West, with some of the greatest volumes in the Pacific Coast States, Idaho, and Montana. Across all woody biomass feedstocks, the Intermountain and Great Plains regions have the least potential supplies.

Increased use of woody biomass for bioenergy is expected to have some ripple effects in the forest and agriculture sectors. Increased use of mill residues for bioenergy will likely decrease their availability for their current use (e.g., oriented strand board, bark mulch, and pellet fuel). Forest residues are currently left in the woods both because they have little product value and, in some management systems, they recycle soil nutrients and improve micro-climate site conditions. There is some evidence that for some sites, removal of harvest residues can reduce soil nutrients, potentially impacting future forest yields. Widespread planting of SRWC for bioenergy feedstock or traditional forest products (e.g., pulpwood) is expected to lead to some reductions in cropland availability for traditional agriculture production. If agriculture yields do not increase as expected in the coming years, this may result in some land transfers from forest to agriculture to increase agriculture production.

There are a number of challenges to increasing the use of woody biomass for bioenergy. Perhaps foremost, woody biomass is not cost competitive with existing fossil fuels, except when generated in large quantities as a waste product. This cost gap may narrow under climate policies where carbon emissions have a market value or the use of woody biomass for bioenergy is promoted. In addition to the economic constraints, there are organizational, infrastructure, and social challenges to widespread implementation of woody biomass for bioenergy. The existing frameworks for energy plant approval and permitting do not always apply well to approval of woody biomass plants. This can make it difficult to establish plants within the energy sector to use woody biomass. There are some concerns that the existing infrastructure (e.g., equipment and transportation systems) is not sufficient to support widespread generation of woody biomass, particularly for a significant expansion in the harvesting of small material from hazard-fuel reduction. Finally, it remains unclear to what extent the public will support significant increases in woody biomass bioenergy production. Opposition by some groups to using biomass for bioenergy is often centered on the belief that energy from wood is outdated technology, the generated energy is inconvenient for use, the feedstock is unreliable and difficult to obtain, and forest resources are better used in the production of other forest products or services.

Additional research is necessary to develop a better understanding of the responses in the energy, agriculture, and forest sectors to policies that would impact bioenergy usage. More comprehensive measurements of both the land suitable for and the willingness to plant SRWC and other energy crops, will help to better identify the potential volumes that could be expected from that resource. Better identification of the locations of current and potential bioenergy production facilities will help to identify those woody biomass resource stocks that may be in the best position for increased use. Similarly, a better understanding of how feedstock (woody and otherwise) supply curves differ by region and subregion will be useful in identifying the locations where woody biomass is most likely to be used for bioenergy.

Glossary of Select Terms

In the text, we have been careful to define important terms and new concepts. However, in this glossary, we provide some definitions of particularly important measurement units and general concepts.

bioenergy—Renewable energy derived from biological sources, to be used for heat, electricity, or vehicle fuel (USDA ERS 2009).

biofuel—Liquid fuels and blending components produced from biomass feed-stocks, used primarily for transportation (US EIA, n.d.).

biomass—Organic nonfossil material of biological origin constituting a renewable energy source (US EIA, n.d.).

British thermal unit (BTU)—Standard unit of measure of the quantity of heat required to raise the temperature of 1 lb of liquid water by 1 degree Fahrenheit at the temperature at which water has its greatest density (approximately 39 degrees Fahrenheit) (US EIA, n.d.). One kilowatt-hour of electricity is equivalent to 3,412 BTUs.

cubic foot of wood—Amount of wood equivalent to a solid cube measuring 12 by 12 by 12 inches (Avery and Burkhart 1994). In this paper, we assume that there are 27.8 dry pounds of woody material in 1 ft^3.

gigawatt hour (GWh)—One billion watt-hours. Often expressed as 1 million kWh.

kilowatt-hour (kWh)—One thousand watt-hours.

megawatt-hour (MWh)—One million watt-hours.

oven dry ton (ODT)—A U.S. ton (2,000 lb, also called a short ton) of biomass material with moisture removed. In this paper, we assume that 1 odt of wood can generate 17.2 million BTUs. A metric ton is equivalent to 1.102 U.S. (or short) tons.

terawatt-hour (TWh)—One trillion watt-hours. Often expressed as 1 billion kWh.

watt—Generally used within the context of capacity of generation or consumption. A unit of electrical power equal to 1 ampere under a pressure of 1 volt. A watt is equal to 1/746 horsepower (US EIA, n.d.).

watt-hour—Electrical energy unit of measure equal to 1 watt of power supplied to, or taken from, an electric circuit steadily for 1 hour (US EIA, n.d.). Typically used in consideration of the amount of electricity generated or consumed. Often expressed in units of 1,000 (i.e., 1 kWh).

Contents

Introduction

A transition from energy based largely on fossil fuels to a greater reliance on renewable energy has been a central focus of many of the current discussions on climate policy. Woody biomass is an important provider of renewable energy currently and is anticipated to be an important component of any future renewable energy portfolio. The current discussion of using woody biomass continues a long history of relying on wood for energy production, both in the United States and in the world. Many technologies currently being discussed for utilizing woody biomass for bioenergy are based on processes established decades ago.

Reflecting the interests of many groups for using woody biomass, the scientific literature, peer-reviewed and grey, on bioenergy from biomass is extensive. Although much of this information is useful, the volume of material available makes a synthesis of the current state of knowledge desirable. Some (e.g., BRDB 2008, Milbrandt 2005, Perlack et al. 2005) have completed syntheses with estimates of available or demanded quantities of woody biomass and agriculture residues. This synthesis differs from those by its economic perspective and reliance on economic models to quantify demands for and supplies of woody biomass. This report also differs from the others by, when possible, considering woody biomass within the context of production quantities and land use changes involving both the agriculture and forest sectors.

The primary goal of this briefing paper is to describe woody biomass feedstocks and examine their potential use in bioenergy production in the context of climate change policy. Specifically, we aim to describe the anticipated uses of biomass for energy production, detail the woody biomass feedstocks and their potential availability, describe general projections of biomass use for bioenergy in the coming decades, and report the results of several economic modeling studies related to the use of woody biomass feedstocks.

In the next section, we discuss some past, current, and expected future uses of woody biomass for bioenergy. We then identify the bioenergy woody biomass feedstocks and provide general estimates of their potential quantities based on the existing literature. Following that general description, we examine a number of studies that modeled the supply and consumption of biomass feedstocks for bioenergy and traditional forest products. We close by describing some of the noneconomic and nontechnical challenges to the increased use of woody biomass for bioenergy.

Woody biomass is anticipated to be an important component of any future renewable energy portfolio.

Context for Considering Bioenergy From Woody Biomass

In the United States in 2008, slightly more than 2.1 quadrillion (10^{15}) BTUs of energy from wood and wood-derived fuels (including black liquor from pulp production) was consumed in all sectors—approximately 8.7 billion cubic feet equivalents of woody material (US EIA 2009a).[1] For comparison, 1.4 quadrillion BTUs of corn and other material was used to produce ethanol in 2008. The component of renewable energy consumption associated with wood and wood-derived fuels has remained fairly constant since 1989 at slightly more than 2 quadrillion BTUs (fig. 1). Over the same period, the amount of energy consumed from wind and biofuels has increased, particularly in the years since 2000.

Within the context of climate change policies, woody biomass is primarily being considered as inputs into three processes: the production of heat, electricity, and biofuels. Woody biomass can also be used to create chemicals not directly used for bioenergy. In the United States in recent decades, the use of woody biomass for the production of heat, electricity, or biofuels has been undertaken as a secondary process to utilize wood residues created in the course of creating other products.

[1] Assuming 17.2 million BTUs per oven dry short ton of wood and 27.8 oven dry pounds per cubic foot.

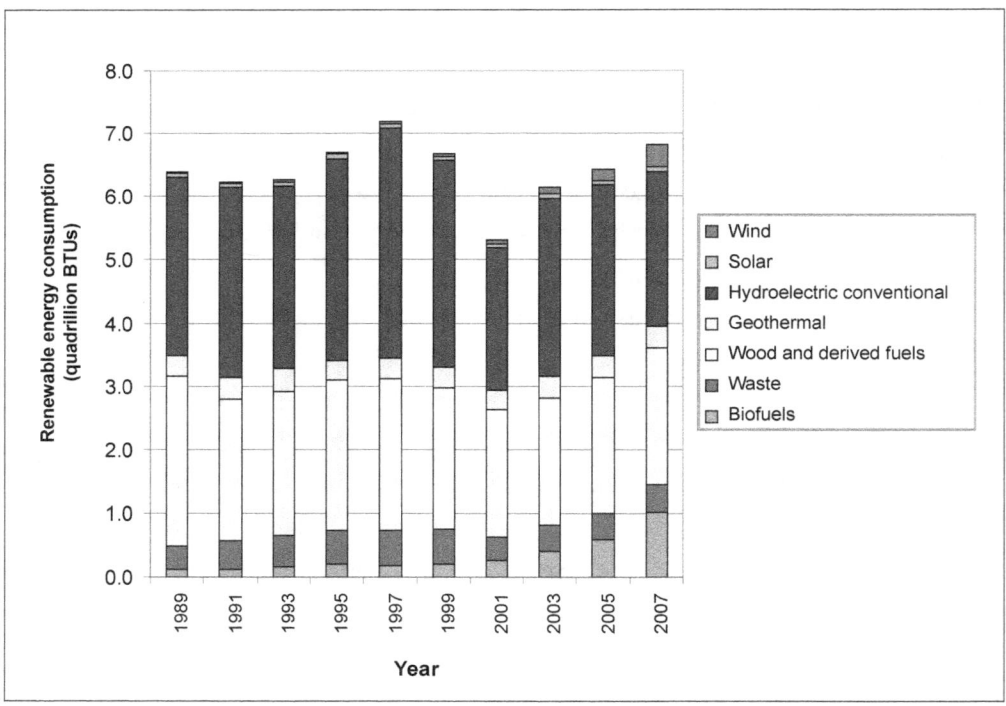

Figure 1—United States energy consumption from renewable sources between 1989 and 2007. Data sources: US EIA 2009b, 2009c.

However, the current expectation is that woody biomass will increasingly be the focus of stand-alone processes where at least some of the biomass is obtained directly from natural resource stocks with the primary intent of generating bioenergy.

Woody biomass has been used to produce either electricity or heat independently as well as in combined heat and power (CHP) systems, also referred to as cogeneration plants. Woody-biomass-fired heat-only operations are often found in Europe, where centralized plants produce heat and hot water that is distributed via piping to local heating districts (see Nicholls et al. 2009 for examples). Small-scale heat-only woody biomass plants have historically been used in the United States to provide heat for drying cut lumber at sawmills and more recently for producing heat for schools (Nicholls et al. 2008). The former operation often relies on milling residues and dirty wood chips, whereas the latter relies on milling residues (e.g., in Vermont) or woody stems harvested as part of hazard-fuel reduction operations (e.g., in Montana) (Nicholls et al. 2008). There is much interest in the United States in taking advantage of significant improvement in efficiency through the use of CHP plants to generate energy from woody biomass. Woody-biomass-fired CHP systems have been implemented in the United States in some institutional settings. However, a challenge to widespread adoption by the electrical sector of CHP plants fired by woody biomass is the general lack in the United States of centralized heating districts (e.g., Maker, n.d.). Space heating using woody biomass in residential and small commercial buildings is typically completed via heat-only wood-burning stoves operating on fuelwood harvested from standing timber or wood pellets made from wood residues.

Electricity-only operations involving woody biomass can rely solely on woody biomass or cofire with another fuel source. If cofired, wood is often combined with coal. Cofiring woody biomass with fuels such as coal can be completed using existing plant technologies with only minor burner tuning and offers an opportunity to directly substitute a renewable fuel for a fossil fuel (Bain and Overend 2002). Additionally, plants originally designed to be fired with coal can be converted to burn woody biomass exclusively, as is being done with two units of the R.E. Berger powerplant in Ohio (FirstEnergy Corporation 2009). Bioelectricity plants using modern technologies were first operated during the 1940s in Oregon using mill residues. More recently, in the 1980s, a number of stand-alone woody-biomass-fired electricity plants came into operation in California. Although there are a number of stand-alone plants where the electricity generated is solely input to the grid, electricity plants operating in association with timber industry are more common. Of the approximately 1,000 wood-fired electricity plants in the United States today,

Woody biomass has been used to produce either electricity or heat independently as well as in combined heat and power systems.

nearly two-thirds are owned and operated by the wood products industry (Nicholls et al. 2008). Much of the electricity generated by industry-owned plants is used onsite rather than contributed to the electrical grid.

In the United States in 2008, 38.8 billion kilowatt-hours (kWh) (38.8 terawatt-hours [TWh]) of electricity were generated using woody biomass. This production represented about 10 percent of the electricity produced from renewable sources (behind hydropower [67 percent of renewable electricity] and wind [14 percent of renewable electricity]) and about 1 percent of all electricity produced (US DOE 2009b). The industrial sector accounted for 27.9 billion kWh of all woody-biomass electricity production—primarily from the wood products sector (US DOE 2009d). Of the 10.9 billion kWh of electricity produced by the electricity-production sector, 2.1 billion kWh were produced from CHP plants (US DOE 2009c)—representing the relative newness of that technology and the scarcity of district heating systems in the United States.

Bioethanol is perhaps the best known biofuel. Methanol and liquid fuels pro-cessed from vegetable oils (e.g., biodiesel) are also biofuels that can be produced using current technology. Bioethanol is desirable because it reduces the need to add octane-enhancers to gasoline, reduces the production of carbon monoxide and hydrocarbons from automobiles by increasing oxygenation of fuel, and offsets the consumption of gasoline produced from fossil fuels (Galbe and Zachhi 2002). One well-documented drawback to producing bioethanol from corn is the creation of competition in demand for corn for food versus energy. In 2007, approximately 24 percent of the corn acreage planted in the United States was used for corn ethanol production (BRDB 2008). In addition to the competition for food production, some have argued that corn ethanol is not a sustainable renewable resource and requires more energy to produce than is contained in ethanol (e.g., Pimentel et al. 2002), although others (e.g., Farrell et al. 2006) have argued against that conclusion.

Corn-based ethanol is considered a first-generation biofuel, whereas commercial-scale cellulosic ethanol production is considered a second-generation technology. Producing ethanol from corn or sugar cane (or other sugar/starch crops) is less technically challenging (and thus currently less costly) than producing ethanol from lignocellulose in woody materials (Galbe and Zachhi 2002, Zerbe 2006). Current ethanol refining capacity in the United States is about 8.5 billion gallons per year with the majority of production achieved from dry milling corn (BRDB 2008). In 2007, the United States produced about 6.5 billion gallons (US DOE, n.d.) and imported about 440 million gallons of ethanol. Cellulosic ethanol can be produced from lignocellulose under several alternative techniques that differ primarily in their approach to hydrolysis (i.e., concentrated acid, diluted acid, or enzymes) of the cellulose to monomer sugars (Galbe and Zachhi 2002). Acid hydrolysis has been used since the 19th century, whereas enzymatic approaches are often the focus of recently developed technologies adopted in new plants (see AE Biofuels Inc. 2008). Contrary to the perception of some that current efforts to produce automotive fuels from wood are novel, liquid fuels were produced from wood in the United States during World War I and in Germany and Switzerland during World War II (Zerbe 2006).

Currently, no commercial-scale cellulosic ethanol plants are operating in the United States; however, several commercial demonstration plants are under construction or have recently begun initial startup. Many of the demonstration plants are supported through funding from the U.S. Department of Energy (DOE) and rely on a variety of feedstocks, including woody biomass. In 2007, DOE provided grants to support a number of commercial-scale cellulosic ethanol plants, having a combined planned capacity of about 130 million gallons of cellulosic ethanol per year (US DOE 2007). Most of these plants are expected to begin startup production in the next couple of years. Only one of the 2007 demonstration plants will solely use woody biomass as a feedstock (40 million gallons/year capacity), and two others (33 million gallons/year capacity in total) will use wood wastes in combination with other feedstocks. One ton of dry woody biomass will produce approximately 89.5 gal of cellulosic ethanol (BRDB 2008). At that conversion rate, producing 20 million gallons of cellulosic ethanol would require about 223,000 oven dry tons (odt) of woody biomass.

Although ethanol receives much of the attention, the production of methanol from wood has also been considered (e.g., Hokanson and Rowell 1977, Zerbe 1991). In recent years, others have promoted producing liquid chemicals (including liquid fuels) and synthetic gas for energy production from black liquor—a byproduct of kraft pulp production (Landalv 2009). Despite long-term interest, the production of methanol from woody biomass has been found to not be economically efficient (e.g., Hokanson and Rowell 1977, Zerbe 1991) and natural gas is currently used to produce most methanol. Much of the black liquor byproduct is currently used to produce heat and electricity for pulp and paper plant operations, and it is yet to be seen if pulp and paper mills will make the capital investments to put biorefinery facilities in place. Although it is technically possible to produce biodiesel from woody biomass, it is generally produced from soybean oil.

In addition to the production of energy, woody biomass from residues or traditionally nonmerchantable material have been used in a variety of products, from visitor information signs (http://altree.com/), to building materials (http://www.fpl.fs.fed.us/documnts/fplgtr/fplgtr110.pdf), to pedestrian bridges (http://www.hdrinc.

com/13/38/1/default.aspx?projectID=582). Woody biomass use for these materials is generally considered in the context of creating value-added products, reducing waste, and creating markets for currently nonmerchantable timber, rather than in consideration of climate change, and we do not consider these products here.

General Projections of Bioenergy Production

The DOE provides estimates of current energy use from renewable sources as well as reference projections to year 2030. In 2008, about 6 percent (6.1 quadrillion BTUs) of the energy consumed in the United States came from renewable sources (excluding ethanol) (US DOE 2009f). For the years 2004 to 2008, about 2.1 quadrillion BTUs of this renewable energy was supplied from woody biomass. Energy consumed from woody biomass accounted for about 30 percent of the renewable energy consumed annually, but just about 2 percent of annual energy consumption from all sources (US DOE 2009a). Renewable energy consumption (excluding ethanol) is projected to increase to 8.4 quadrillion BTUs (8 percent of energy consumption) by 2015 and to 9.7 quadrillion BTUs (9 percent) by 2030. Assuming the current share of renewable energy coming from woody biomass remains static, woody biomass would be the source of about 2.5 quadrillion BTUs of energy in 2015 and 2.9 quadrillion BTUs of energy in 2030. At present, wood energy consumption requires about 122 million odt of woody material annually (assuming 17.2 million BTUs per odt of wood). Under the reference projection from the DOE, approximately 145 million odt of wood will be used for energy in 2015 and 168 million odt will be used in 2030.

The Renewable Fuels Standard (RFS) of the Energy Independence and Security Act of 2007 requires increased production of ethanol, including significant expansion of advanced biofuel production. By 2022, the RFS targets that 36 billion gallons of ethanol be used, with 21 billion gallons of that coming in the form of advanced biofuels, including at least 16 billion gallons of cellulosic ethanol. Although no commercial-scale production facilities for cellulosic ethanol are currently in place, several should begin initial production in the next several years. At least one of these plants (the Range Fuels plant in Soperton, Georgia) is focused solely on the production of cellulosic ethanol and methanol from woody biomass. Any wood biomass demanded to support the RFS is in addition to that identified above in the baseline DOE projections.

In examining increased cellulosic ethanol production, the Biomass Research and Development Board (BRDB) (2008) assumed conservatively that 4 billion gallons of cellulosic ethanol would come from woody material in support of meeting the RFS in 2022. At 89.5 gallons of ethanol per odt of wood using expected technologies, this production would require about 45 million odt of wood. At a price of $44/odt, approximately 45 percent (20 million odt) of the forest resource feedstock is expected to come from logging residues, 25 percent (11 million odt) from thinnings for hazard-fuel reduction, and 14 percent (6 million odt) from other forest resource removals for such things as land clearing. The remainder is expected to come from mill residues (3 percent), municipal wood waste (5 percent), and material that might otherwise be used for conventional wood production (8 percent). The projected use of 45 million dry tons of woody material for cellulosic ethanol production serves as a useful baseline for expected future demand for woody material for biofuels.

Congress is currently considering a renewable electricity standard (RES) to increase the production of electricity generated from renewable sources. Although the proposed legislation has yet to be formally presented, it is reasonable to expect the RES would lead to at least some increase in electricity generation from woody biomass over any baseline increases. The DOE reference projections for electricity (which do not include an RES) can provide a projection of the baseline expectations for future renewable electricity generation from biomass. In 2008, approximately 43 billion kWh (43 TWh) of electricity was generated from wood and other biomass, most of which was woody biomass (US DOE 2009e). The current level of electricity production is estimated to require about 30 million odt of woody material.[2] Because the majority of the woody biomass electricity is generated by the forest products sector, much of the material currently used to generate electricity likely comes from mill residues, both woody and black liquor. The DOE projects that electricity generation from wood and other biomass will increase to 81 billion kWh by 2105 and 218 billion kWh by 2030 (fig. 2). These projected figures include expected expansion of the biomass supply from energy crops—including perennial grasses and energy cane—grown on agriculture lands. Assuming the share of woody biomass contribution to renewable electricity and electricity generation efficiency from woody biomass remains constant, approximately 57 million odt of woody biomass will be demanded in 2015 and 154 million odt of woody material in 2030 for electricity generation. Efficiency improvements would reduce the volume of material required. The establishment of an RES would likely lead to an increase over this baseline.

Bioenergy Production and Carbon Policies

The reference projections from the DOE indicate a general increase in the extent of energy created from biomass in the decades ahead. Policies aimed at reducing carbon

---

[2] Assuming approximately 0.7 oven dry tons of woody biomass per megawatt hour.

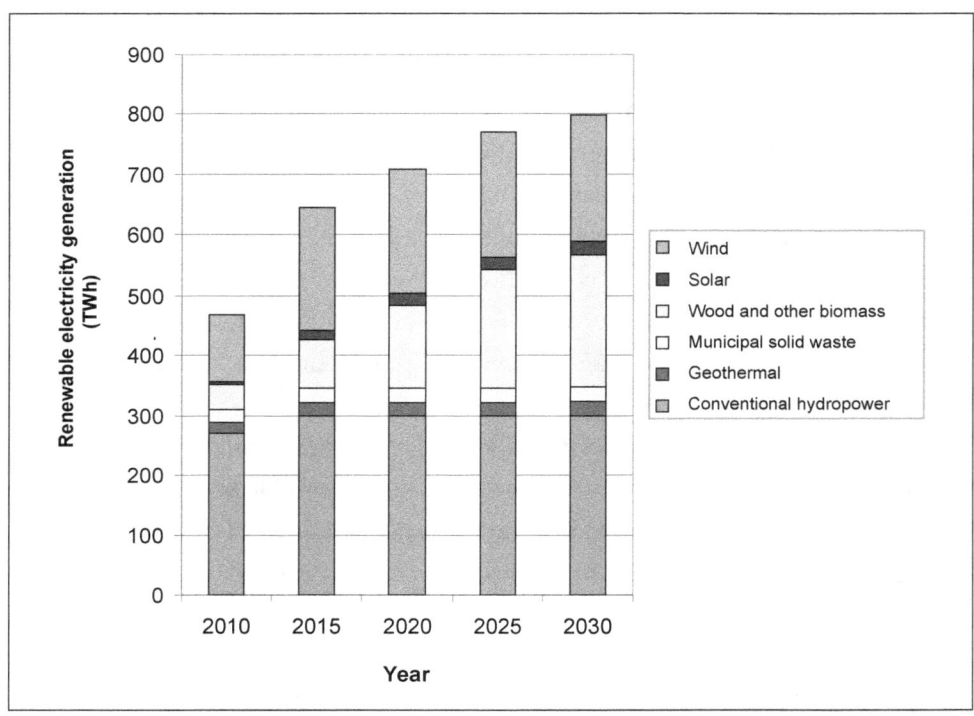

Figure 2—Projected baseline electricity generation from renewable fuel sources, 2010 to 2030. Data source: US DOE 2009e.

emissions are expected to increase use of woody biomass for energy generation because it results in less carbon emissions than using coal (although greater than natural gas). Johansson and Azar (2007) examined the impact of a carbon tax or cap and trade system on U.S. bioenergy and agricultural production. In the Johansson and Azar model, bioenergy feedstock was available from energy crops grown on cropland and grazing land and from agriculture and forestry residues. Under a policy where carbon is highly valued at $50/ton in 2010 and increasing linearly to $800/ton in 2100 and with no carbon offset opportunities, biomass is expected to be the source of about 16 percent of the energy generated in the United States in 2030—approximately a fourfold increase over modeled use in the current period. Johansson and Azar (2007) projected that by 2050, biomass would be the source of about 30 percent of the energy generated—approximately a sevenfold increase from the modeled use in the current period. In both future years, the projected biomass use levels are approximately double those projected by the DOE in their reference case. In the Johansson and Azar model, where carbon has a high value, coal use begins to decline dramatically in 2020 and falls out of energy production by 2070. It is important to note that Johansson and Azar did not include carbon offsets, which are likely to be an important tool for coal powerplants to meet carbon caps under the legislation currently being considered in the U.S. Congress.

Changes in crop mix and agricultural land uses are expected under a carbon policy. The Johansson and Azar model does not include a forest sector, so land use change between forests and agriculture was not modeled. For the agriculture sector, a carbon policy that creates a carbon price of between $20 and $40/ton leads to a conversion of up to 24 million acres of cropland to produce biomass for bioenergy (Johansson and Azar 2007, estimated from sensitivity analysis results). At carbon prices higher than $40/ton, high-quality grazing land begins to be used for energy crop production. At a $50/ton carbon price, about 24 million acres of cropland and 49 million acres of high-quality grazing lands would be devoted to energy crop production. At carbon prices above $150/ton, low-quality grazing land begins to be converted to energy crop production. Despite having fewer acres in energy crop production, cropland provided most of the energy crop volume from agriculture lands because of higher yields. Under the simulated carbon policy, farm prices for energy crops are projected to increase to more than $30/ton in 2020 and to about $50/ton in 2040 (Johansson and Azar 2007).

Woody Biomass Feedstocks

Woody biomass for use in bioenergy and biofuel production is generally considered from the following sources: short-rotation woody crops (SRWC), residues from timber harvests that would typically be left onsite (either dispersed or in piles), residues from the milling process that may or may not already be used in other processes, waste wood and yard debris collected via municipal solid waste systems, timber resources that could be harvested for other products (e.g., saw logs or pulpwood), and stems that are currently considered nonmerchantable (including those that could be harvested in the course of forest management activities).

Some woody biomass materials are available to the bioenergy production process cost free or at very low cost. In the case of a few woody biomass feedstocks, their use for bioenergy may avoid disposal costs (e.g., avoided waste hauling costs). Other biomass materials are available to the bioenergy production processes only if procured and transported. Those biomass products that are low-cost or no-cost to procure (e.g., milling residues, black liquor) are already widely used for the production of energy (including through wood pellets) or other wood products (e.g., oriented strand board, bark mulch). Other forms of woody biomass expensive to procure (e.g., nonmerchantable stems) or that are currently not widely produced (e.g., SRWC) might become widely used only after additional investment in their production (e.g., extensive planting of SRWC), increased yields, increased prices of fossil fuels, and/or increased support for bioenergy production.

Biomass products that are low-cost or no-cost to procure are already widely used for the production of energy or other wood products.

Four "types" of availability have typically been reported in woody biomass studies completed to date. Some studies (e.g., Milbrandt 2005) report all or nearly all of the quantity of woody biomass as "potentially available." Other studies (e.g., Perlack et al. 2005), report the amount of biomass that is "technically available" and could be used. This has generally been accomplished by applying a percentage factor, representing the amount of biomass that is expected to be recoverable using current or expected technology, to the potentially available quantity of woody biomass. A smaller number of studies have quantified the amount of woody biomass that could be available at a given market price (e.g., BRDB 2008, Walsh et al. 2003). Finally, a few studies have estimated a supply curve, a schedule of supplied quantities over a range of prices, for woody biomass (e.g., Gan 2007, Walsh et al. 2000). In various places in this report, we rely on each type of "availability" and make an effort to differentiate these types for the reader.

Short-Rotation Woody Crops

Short-rotation woody crops are tree crops grown on short rotations, typically with more intensive management than timber plantations. All of the studies described here considered SRWC grown strictly on agriculture land. However, it is possible that SRWC could be planted on land currently in forest plantations or naturally regenerated forests. The tree species most commonly considered as SRWC are hybrid poplars (*Populus* spp.) and willow (*Salix* spp.)—although sycamore (*Platanus* spp.) and silver maple (*Acer saccharinum* L.) have also been considered (Tuskan 1998). Short-rotation woody crops are one component of a larger group of plantings known as energy crops, which also include the perennials switchgrass (*Panicum virgatum* L.) and energy cane (high-sugar varieties of sugar cane [*Saccharum* L.])— both of which are also typically planted on agriculture land. In addition to their potential use for bioenergy and biofuel, SRWC can also be used for pulp and paper production and sawtimber (Rinebolt 1996, Stanton et al. 2002). In the 1970s oil embargo, SRWC were considered as a potential biofuel source (Stanton et al. 2002). During most of the period since then and until recent years, the primary interest in SRWC has been as a quick-growing high-yield timber supply (Tuskan 1998).

Rotation lengths for SRWC range from about 6 to 12 years, although they can be shorter (3 years, e.g., Adegbidi et al. 2001) if the material is sold for bioenergy feedstock or longer (up to 15 years, e.g., Stanton et al. 2002) if sold for sawtimber. As with timber harvests on forest land, multiple products can be derived from harvested SRWC stands, with stems being used for clean chips for pulp and paper and limbs and other residues being sold for energy (Schmidt 2006). Some studies have assumed that 25 percent of the material harvested from SRWC stands (mostly bark and small limbs) can be sold for energy with the remainder going to higher valued products (e.g., McCarl et al. 2000). Harvested SRWC stands can be regenerated via stump coppicing or planting of new cuttings. Stump coppicing reduces the cost of regeneration, but coppicing can add to labor costs when thinning of the coppice sprouts is required. Regeneration through stump coppicing also requires alternate harvest timing and can result in missed opportunities to take advantage of genetic improvements in new planting stock (Stanton et al. 2002, Tuskan 1998). Coppice regeneration is more common when the stand will be harvested for bioenergy production (e.g., Adegbidi et al. 2001). Coppiced willow may ultimately be the most popular crop for bioenergy production under low-price bioenergy feedstock scenarios (Ince and Moiseyev 2002).

SRWC acreage—

The number of acres currently planted in SRWC is not definitively known, although the total acreage is not extensive (Tuskan 1998). Ince (2009) estimated that less than 0.1 percent of the privately owned agriculture and forest land base is currently dedicated to SRWC poplar plantations. Zalesny (2008), citing the work of Eaton (2007), reports approximately 132,000 ac of hybrid poplar currently planted in the United States. Hybrid poplar is planted on approximately 50,000 ac in the Pacific Northwest—for pulpwood and sawtimber production—(Stanton et al. 2002) and on about 6,000 ac in Minnesota for both pulpwood and energy production. Short-rotation woody crops have also been planted in the South (Tuskan 1998) and the Northeast (including willow for bioelectricity production) (Adegbidi et al. 2001). It is expected that expansion of the market for bioenergy feedstocks would support significant expansion of SRWC acreage on marginal to good agriculture lands (Wright et al. 1992). Alig et al. (2000) assumed that about 170 million acres of cropland was physically suitable for planting SRWC, mostly in the Corn Belt, Lake States, and South Central states (table 1).

Table 1—Cropland suitable for short-rotation woody crop planting

Region	Area
	Thousand acres
Pacific Northwest	1,274
Lake States	33,190
Corn Belt	85,040
Southeast	14,022
South Central	36,816

Source: Alig et al. 2000.

SRWC yields—

Current estimates of expected yields from SRWC come from limited numbers of stands planted on a variety of sites in different regions of the country using different planting stocks. However, general yield figures for SRWC using contemporary planting stock under current management systems range from 5 to 12 dry tons per acre per year of woody material (Adegbidi et al. 2001, BRDB 2008, Volk et al. 2006). Under 6-year rotations with 900 trees per acre, Stanton et al. (2002) reported yields from hybrid poplar planted for bioenergy of 37 to 55 dry tons per acre at the time of harvest. Under a management regime aimed primarily at using SRWC for pulpwood production, stem densities of 600 trees per acre yielded 28 to 45 dry tons per acre of clean chips for pulpwood and an additional 10 to 15 dry tons of dirty chips for bioenergy production. In the Pacific Northwest, hybrid poplar grown for saw-log production is estimated to yield up to 12 dry tons per acre of chips for energy production at the time of harvest (Stanton et al. 2002).

Biomass From Harvest Residues

Harvest residues are the unused portions of growing-stock trees (e.g., tops, limbs, stems, and stumps) that are cut or killed by harvesting operations and currently left onsite (Smith et al. 2009). Harvest residues may be left distributed across the harvesting site or may be piled. In some management systems, harvest residues are mulched (e.g., in the South and on gentle slopes in the West) or burned (e.g., in the Pacific Northwest), whereas in other systems the residues are left distributed throughout the harvest site to naturally decay. In 2006, approximately 4.6 billion cubic feet of harvest residues were generated (Smith et al. 2009). The reported volume of harvest residues has been increasing since the 1950s (Smith et al. 2009); however, this increase is influenced to at least some extent by changes in reporting and sampling systems. In addition to the residues from harvesting operations, some studies (e.g., Perlack et al. 2005) also consider the residue generated in "other removals," which include forest harvests conducted for activities like land clearing and precommercial thinnings. In 2006, there was approximately 1.6 billion cubic feet of woody material in "other removals" (Smith et al. 2009).

Assuming 27.8 dry pounds of material per cubic foot, the harvest residues in 2006 amount to about 64 million dry tons of cut or killed material left on harvest sites. Only a portion of this material would be available for use in the production of bioenergy or biofuel given current technology and costs of handling and transport. In their report, Perlack et al. (2005) assumed that it was technically feasible to remove about 65 percent of harvest residue, equating to about 42 million dry tons of residue in 2006. The spatial distribution of harvest residues in the United States

---

In 2006, approximately 4.6 billion cubic feet of harvest residues were generated.

generally follows the spatial distribution of harvests, with the South (2.3 billion cubic feet) and the North (1.3 billion cubic feet) accounting for the majority of the residue generated (fig. 3).

Harvest residues, regional availability—

The amount of harvest residues that are economically available is less than the amount technically available (measured in Perlack et al. 2005). With the goal of producing 4 billion gallons of cellulosic ethanol from a combination of woody biomass feedstocks, BRDB (2008) estimated that about 20 million dry tons of forest residues would be supplied annually from nonfederal timberlands at a roadside price of $44 per dry ton. Counties in the southern Delta region, the Northeast, along the Pacific Coast, and in the northern Lake States were projected to have the greatest quantities of forest biomass supplied (BRDB 2008). Counties in the Mountain West would have the least forest residue supplied.

Regionally, the Northeast and the hardwood producing areas of the upper Midwest would seem to have the greatest opportunity for increased use of timber

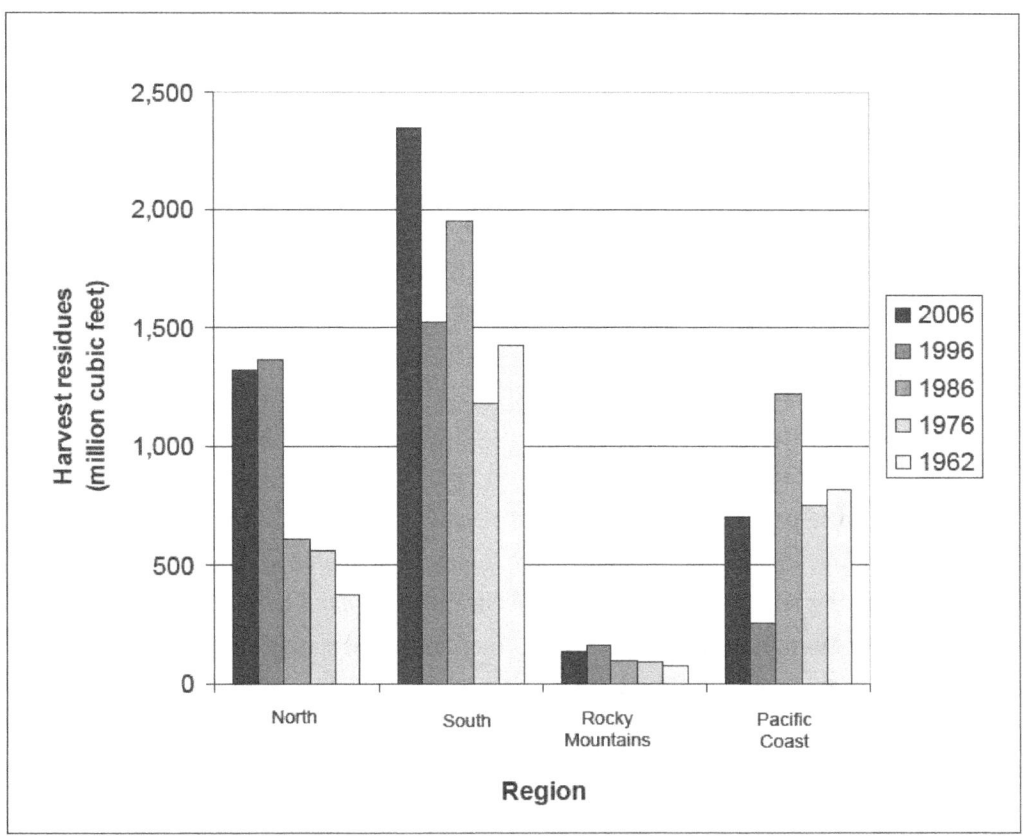

Figure 3—Harvest residues generated in the United States by region, 1962 to 2006. Data source: Smith et al. 2009.

harvest residues given the current volume generated per harvest acre, all else being equal. However, the South generates the greatest volumes of residue owing to high harvesting rates. The predominance of coal-fired powerplants in the East may offer opportunities to cofire harvest residue woody biomass. The existing infrastructure for producing corn ethanol and the nascent infrastructure for cellulosic ethanol in some parts of the Midwest may be a catalyst for establishment of harvest residue feedstock use in that region.

One uncertainty for the Northeast and Midwest in regard to expanding harvest residue use for bioenergy is any significant shifts in forest species composition in response to climate change. There is the potential that climate change may result in the movement north to Canada of hardwood species and a northward progression of Southern U.S. softwood species. Timber harvests involving softwoods tend to generate fewer residues than harvests involving hardwoods (Smith et al. 2009). Furthermore, the amount of residues generated and left onsite in softwood harvesting operations has declined over the last several decades (Smith et al. 2009). The increased utilization of harvested softwood reflects both technological improvements in softwood harvesting systems as well as additional markets for softwood biomass. At the same time, the volume of softwood harvested nationally has been declining since about 1976. Hardwood harvests have declined in recent periods but are still greater than 1976 and 1986 volumes (Smith et al. 2009).

Harvest residues, harvest site implications—
In management systems where harvest residues have traditionally been left onsite, removing all harvest residues can have implications for soil nutrients and soil carbon. This can lead to reductions in tree growth in subsequent rotations (e.g., Walmsley et al. 2009). However, the impact of whole-tree harvest on soil nutrients and growth in the second rotation is highly variable and likely site specific (Carter et al. 2006, Walmsley et al. 2009). If removal of logging residues led to widespread reductions in future timber yields, timber supplies could decline, leading to increased stumpage prices and timberland values, all else being equal. Alternately, managers may choose to use fertilizer to augment available soil nutrients on areas where logging residues have been removed. This may lead to increased fertilizer use, which might have implications for greenhouse gas emissions and water quality. Ultimately, the widespread impact, if any, of a general shift to removing logging residues from harvesting operations is not known and would require careful monitoring in the future. One potential benefit from whole-tree harvesting is that it can reduce site preparation costs for subsequent timber rotations (Westbrook et al. 2007).

Biomass From Milling Residues

Milling residues include wastes from sawdust, slabs and edgings, bark, veneer clippings, and black liquor (Rinebolt 1996). In 2006, woody biomass milling residues from primary wood processing mills amounted to approximately 87 million dry tons of material (Smith et al. 2009). This is up slightly from the 83 million dry tons of milling residue generated in 2001 (Smith et al. 2003). Black liquor production is not considered here. Reflecting their low cost of procurement (or avoided cost of disposal) nearly all milling residues—about 86 million dry tons—are currently used in production of other products or bioenergy. This pattern of use continues a practice in place since about 1986 (Rinebolt 1996). In 2006, nearly equal amounts of residues (36 million dry tons) were used for energy production and fiber products with an additional 13 million dry tons used for other products (Smith et al. 2009). Some (e.g., Perlack et al. 2005, Rinebolt 1996) suggested there may be increased availability of milling residues in the future, assuming increased timber mill production (e.g., in response to hazard-fuel thinning). However, this seems to ignore the pattern of increasing efficiency in timber mill production practices over past decades, which has been projected to continue in the future (Skog 2007). If robust markets for woody biomass for bioenergy and biofuel develop in the future, the delivered prices for woody biomass could draw some milling residues from the production of other products to bioenergy and biofuel production. This would likely then lead to at least short-term increases in the costs of products currently produced from milling residues.

Reflecting their low cost of procurement, nearly all milling residues are currently used in production of other products or bioenergy.

Mill residues, regional availability—

The South Central and Northeast regions have the greatest volume of milling residues not currently used (fig. 4). Most of this unused residue is in the form of slabs, edgings, and trimmings (i.e., coarse material). This could be fortuitous, as the Northeast generates a significant amount of electricity from coal and would likely have an opportunity to expand cofiring of woody residues with coal. However, even in the South Central and Northeast regions, the amount of unused residue is small. Woody biomass supplied from SRWC may offer a greater long-term opportunity for cofiring woody biomass with coal than do milling residues.

Mill residues, secondary wood product facilities—

Mill residues created at secondary wood product manufacturing facilities (e.g., cabinet production, furniture makers) are another mill residue source. Unfortunately, the amount of woody material available from secondary wood processing industries is difficult to ascertain. Milbrandt (2005) estimated approximately 3 million tons of woody residues are generated annually from secondary wood product firms. In

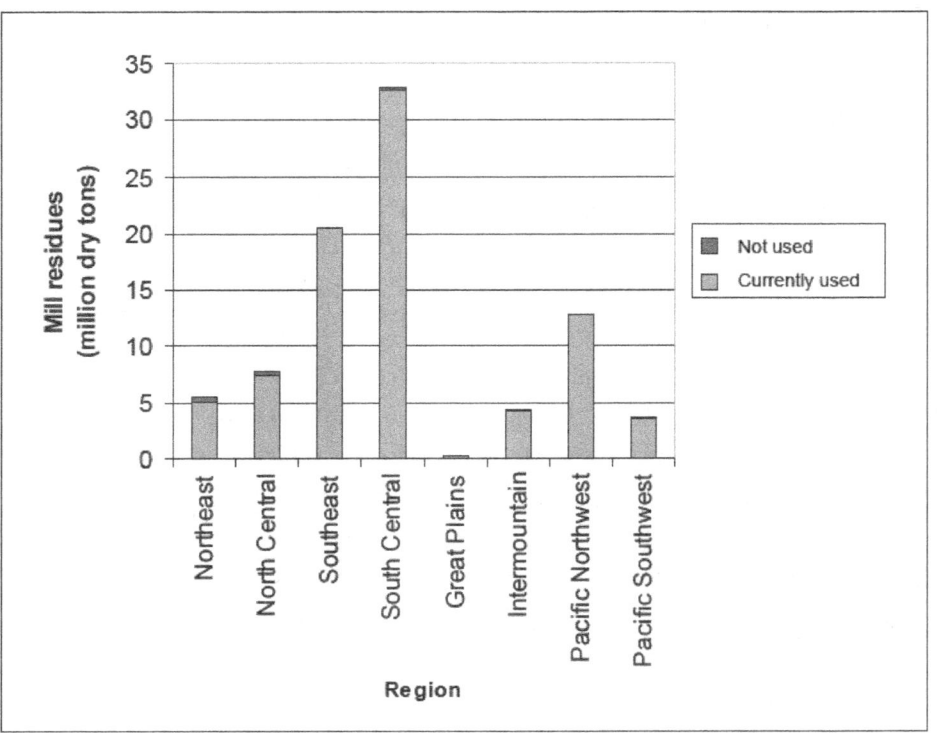

Figure 4—Woody biomass mill residues generated in the United States, 2006. Data source: Smith et al. 2009.

a previous study completed in the late 1990s, approximately 1 million dry tons of secondary mill residues were estimated to be available annually for feedstock use at approximately $20 per ton (1996 dollars) (Rooney 1998). Although potentially available residues from secondary mills are distributed throughout the forested regions of the country, they represent a fraction of the other potentially available woody material. Further, as the secondary wood products manufacturing industry continues to contract (Quesada and Gazo 2006), the amount of residue available will likely also decline. Ultimately, secondary wood product residue is perhaps best characterized as a niche source of woody biomass for bioenergy and biofuel production in some locales.

Municipal and Construction/Demolition Wastes

Wood and paperboard in a variety of consumer products are discarded as municipal solid waste (MSW). A portion of that waste is recovered for recycling or other uses, and the remainder is generally discarded into landfills. In MSW, woody biomass can be found in paperboard and paper waste, discarded wood products such as furniture, durable goods, crates and packaging, and in yard trimmings. In 2007, the United States generated approximately 83 million tons of paper and paperboard—54.5 percent (45 million tons) of this was recovered for recycling or other uses (US EPA 2008). Corrugated boxes make up the greatest single component of the paper and paperboard waste stream and, after newspapers, the highest rate of product recovery. The generation of paper and paperboard waste has flattened in recent years after a decades-long increase. Over the same period, the rate of recovery of this waste has continued to increase (US EPA 2008). Discarded wood in furniture, durable goods, and wood packaging amounted to 14.2 million tons in 2007. An estimated 1.3 million tons of discarded wood from pallets was recovered for such things as mulch and animal bedding. Yard wastes are difficult to measure, but disposal is believed to have declined from highs in the early 1990s in response to legislation limiting yard waste disposal in landfills (US EPA 2008). In 2007, about 6 million tons of brush and leaves were generated but not recovered from yard debris. Including paper and paperboard, approximately 57 million tons of woody biomass is currently discarded and not currently recovered. Excluding paper and paperboard, approximately 19 million tons of wood is not recovered from the MSW stream. In both instances, one could expect that only a portion of this material is recoverable for use in the production of bioenergy and biofuels. Perlack et al. (2005) estimated that approximately 7.7 million tons of solid wood was available from MSW.

In addition to that contained in MSW, discarded solid wood is potentially available in the debris created from building construction and demolition. Between 20 and 30 percent of construction and demolition debris is estimated to be solid wood products (e.g., dimension lumber, wood doors and flooring, wood shingles) (US EPA 2009). In 2003, approximately 164 million tons of debris material was created from construction and demolition (US EPA 2009). Assuming 25 percent of that material was wood, approximately 41 million tons of wood waste was created from construction and demolition in 2003. This is very similar to a previous estimate of 39 million tons of debris wood in 2002 from McKeever (2004). McKeever (2004) has estimated that approximately 50 percent of construction and demolition wood waste is potentially recoverable or currently recovered. Assuming this percentage, almost 20 million tons of wood was available from construction and demolition debris in 2003.

Biomass From Hazard-Fuel Reduction

Much of the material on public and private forests identified as overstocked or at high risk of fire because of stand conditions is small-diameter material for which there is not currently a market. With no market for this precommercial material, there is limited opportunity to offset the costs of thinning these forested stands. With renewed attention to bioenergy, there is much interest in using the precommercial material in hazard-fuel treatments as woody material feedstock for bioenergy and biofuel production (e.g., WGA 2006). The focus of hazard-fuel treatments is the Western United States, and Skog et al. (2006, 2008) identified approximately 24 million acres in the 12 Western States on all ownership types as potential sites for treatment. This acreage figure compares well with the 28 million acres of timberland in 15 Western States likely to need mechanical fuel treatment as identified by Rummer et al. (2005).

Hazard fuel reduction, potential biomass—
Skog et al. (2006, 2008) simulated both even-age and uneven-age thinning operations. The uneven-age scenarios included two aimed at achieving high structural diversity in the remaining stand and two aimed at achieving limited structural diversity in the remaining stand. In the uneven-age scenarios, stems in a variety of diameters were removed. In the even-age scenarios, larger diameter stems were removed only if all smaller diameter stems had been removed (thin from below). No diameter limits were included in the scenarios. Some scenarios had limits on the amount of basal area that could be removed in the thinning. In all cases, acres were deemed treatable only if they would provide 300 ft^3 of merchantable material per acre—a volume that is often considered the minimum necessary to yield net revenue (Skog et al. 2006, 2008).

> **The majority of the simulated removed biomass material from hazard-fuel reduction is associated with timberland on national forests.**

Scenarios that treat acres using an uneven-age management thinning regime aimed at maintaining high structural diversity and containing no limits on basal area removed yielded the greatest number of acres treatable—17.5 million acres—and material removed—627 million odt (Skog et al. 2006, 2008). An even-age thinning from below with no basal area limits was estimated to be feasible on about 7.3 million acres, yielding about 190 million odt of material. Fewer acres are treatable under the even-age regime because lesser amounts of merchantable material would be generated in the treatment, making this regime feasible only under limited conditions. In the uneven-age management regime, about 35 percent of the removed material would come from California timberlands (fig. 5). Oregon, Idaho, and Montana timberlands each would account for an additional 13 percent of removed material. The remaining approximately 25 percent of material would come mostly from Washington, Colorado, and New Mexico.

Westwide across all scenarios, the majority (approximately 55 percent) of the simulated removed biomass material from hazard-fuel reduction is associated with timberland on national forests (Skog et al. 2006, 2008). Under an example uneven-age thinning regime aimed at achieving limited structural diversity and with a basal area limit, privately owned lands would contribute approximately 32 percent of removed biomass (122 million odt of merchantable and nonmerchantable material) (table 2). Of the private timberland in Western States, those in California would contribute the greatest volume (50 million odt) of thinned material under this thinning

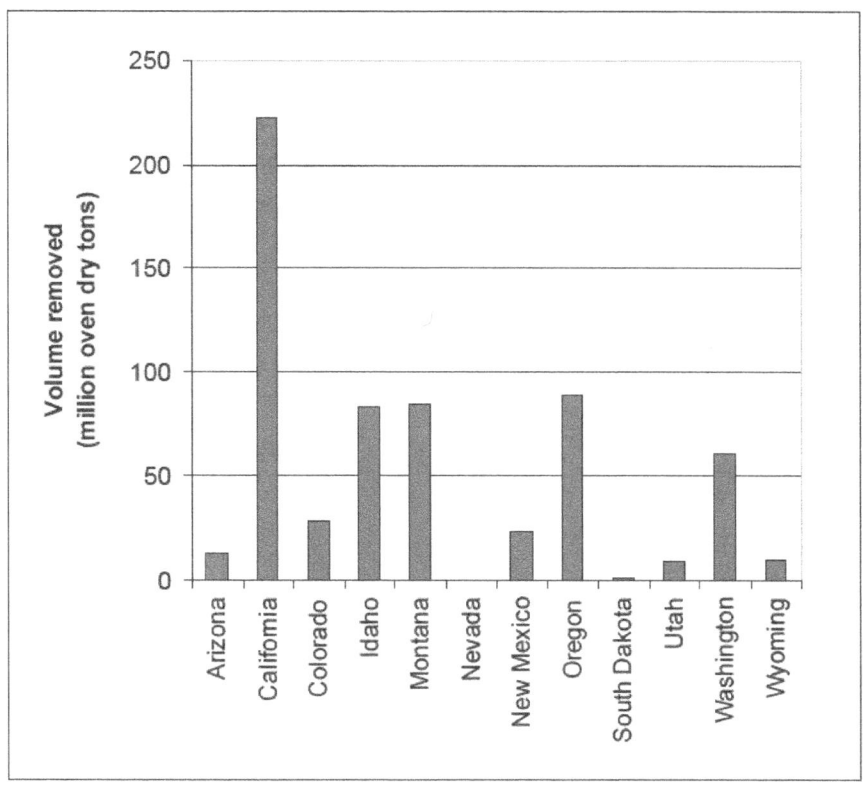

Figure 5—Material of all sizes removed from a simulated uneven-age thinning regime on public and private timberland in the Western States. Data source: Adapted from Skog et al. 2006.

regime. The contribution of material from private timberlands would be lowest (less than 4 million odt) in Arizona, Nevada, New Mexico, South Dakota, Utah, and Wyoming because of small areas of timberland in those states.

An uneven-age thinning regime without basal area limits and promoting high structural diversity would yield about 9.5 odt per acre of material from stems less than 7 inches in diameter and from the branches and tops of stems used for higher value products (Skog et al. 2006). This material is most likely to be used for bioenergy production. Treatment on all 17.5 million acres where this uneven-age thinning regime is feasible would yield about 166 million odt of small woody material. The thinning-from-below even-age regime would yield approximately 11 odt per acre of material from stems less than 7 inches in diameter and the branches and tops of stems used for higher value products (Skog et al. 2006). If all 7.3 million even-age feasible acres were treated, about 80 million odt of small woody material could be generated. In both cases, it is unlikely that all of this material would be harvested at once. Assuming operations occur evenly over approximately 20 years (i.e., 2010 to 2030) with no retreatment, about 8.3 million odt could be removed per year under the former scenario and 4 million odt per year under the latter scenario. This is a

Table 2—Volume of material removed under a simulated uneven-age hazard-fuel thinning regime by timberland ownership type

State	Private	National forest	Other federal	State and local	Total
		Million oven dry tons (odt)			
Arizona	2.0	6.9	0.0	0.0	8.9
California	50.0	65.1	0.6	1.7	117.4
Colorado	5.9	8.9	2.4	0.2	17.4
Idaho	13.2	35.7	3.5	5.3	57.7
Montana	14.8	38.2	3.2	2.6	58.9
Nevada	0.2	0.0	0.0	0.0	0.2
New Mexico	3.3	10.7	0.0	1.1	15.0
Oregon	16.3	28.3	8.4	2.1	55.1
South Dakota	0.0	1.1	0.0	0.0	1.1
Utah	1.6	3.9	0.3	1.1	6.9
Washington	12.8	18.4	1.1	6.4	38.8
Wyoming	2.3	3.1	1.8	0.1	7.3
Total	122.3	220.2	21.3	20.8	384.6

Source: Adapted from Skog et al. 2006.

slight simplification, as it ignores stand growth over that period, which may move some stems into higher valued uses and ignores the growth of new small-diameter material.

Perlack et al. (2005) reported that 49 million dry tons of woody biomass could be generated from timberland through hazard-fuel harvests throughout the country annually. Perlack et al. estimated an additional 11 million dry tons available from forest lands (lands not productive enough to be classified as timberland) annually. The vast majority of this volume is expected to be generated in the Western States. The results of the two studies provide good sideboards on likely woody biomass availability. The study by Perlack et al. (2005) contains a fairly liberal set of assumptions on likely treatable acres and generated volume. Skog et al. (2006) adopted a fairly stringent set of assumptions on treatable acres, including the requirement of producing at least 300 ft^3 of merchantable material. The results of Skog et al. (2006) likely provide a more reasonable estimate of the potential production from hazard-fuel thinnings. This is particularly true in the short run where institutions are not in place to support widespread hazard-reduction thinning, markets currently support only low prices for bioenergy chips, and there are a number of social obstacles to thinning for bioenergy.

The results reported in Skog et al. (2006, 2008) are consistent with the analysis (involving many of the same authors) reported by the Western Governors Association on forest biomass availability (WGA 2006). In that analysis, 10.6 million acres of western timberland is available for hazard fuel reduction yielding 270 million odt of biomass. Assuming these acres were treated over a 22-year period and that 50 percent of the removed biomass could potentially be available for bioenergy and biofuel production, the annual volume of available woody biomass would be 6.2 million odt. Again, this figure is well below that reported in Perlack et al. (2005).

Hazard-fuel reduction, costs and revenues—
Mechanical treatment and removal to the roadside is an expensive approach to treating hazard fuels. In general, treating the fuels via prescribed burning is less expensive (Rummer et al. 2005), although the resulting reductions in fire hazard may not be similar to that achieved via mechanical thinning. Mechanical treatment and removal to the roadside is estimated to have an average cost of between $34/odt and $86/odt for a variety of western forest types on a mix of site types (Rummer et al. 2005) (table 3). These treatment costs do not include the additional costs for hauling the removed material from the roadside to the mill. Treatment costs are strongly influenced by site conditions, and treatments on slopes greater than 40 percent are estimated to cost at least double that of treatments on gentle slopes (Skog et al. 2006).

The uncertainty around whether hazard-fuel reduction could generate net revenues per acre is a challenge to widespread implementation of hazard thinning. For a simulated uneven-age thinning regime, Skog et al. (2006) estimated treatment and removal to the roadside would cost on average about $27/odt on gentle slopes and $51/odt on slopes greater than 40 percent. A typical delivered value assumed for dirty chips for energy production is $30/odt. Based on those costs and values, and if all material is used for dirty chips, there is a **net cost** of about $21/odt at the roadside for treatment on slopes greater than 40 percent and a small **net revenue** of about $3 at the roadside on gentle slopes (fig. 6). The $3 of net revenue on gentle

> **Mechanical treatment and removal to the roadside is estimated to have an average cost of between $34/odt and $86/odt for a variety of western forest types.**

Table 3—Treatment costs for removal and transportation to the roadside of hazard fuels

Forest type	Costs
	Dollars/odt
Southwest ponderosa pine	55.74
Intermountain ponderosa pine	55.26
Intermountain lodgepole pine	45.24
Sierras ponderosa pine	44.78
Sierras lodgepole pine	57.85
Rocky Mountain ponderosa pine	61.46
Rocky Mountain lodgepole pine	48.91
Great Basin ponderosa pine	86.96
Great Basin lodgepole pine	34.72

Note: odt = oven dry ton.
Source: Adapted from Rummer et al. 2005.

slopes is prior to incurring transport costs to the processing site. At an assumed transportation cost of 35 cents per mile, in this example roadside net revenues would be negated after an 8.5 mi transport to the processing facility.

Based on the expected costs and delivered values, it is unlikely that hazard-fuel treatment could widely be economically feasible if all removed material is required to be sold for energy chips. In their study, after accounting for expected transport costs, Skog et al. (2006) found that no simulated hazard-fuel thinning regime yielded net revenue per acre if all woody material was required to be sold for chips at $30/odt (table 4). However, if some of the thinned material could be sold for higher valued pulp and sawtimber products, some thinning regimes became economically feasible. When stems above 7 inches in diameter can be sold for higher valued products, uneven-age thinning regimes conducted on gentle slopes yield net revenue (table 4). However, even-age thinning regimes and any thinning regime conducted on steep slopes did not yield net revenue even if material was sold for higher valued products (table 4). Under a scenario where energy chip value increased by $20 (e.g., through a subsidy or as a reflection of increased demand), all

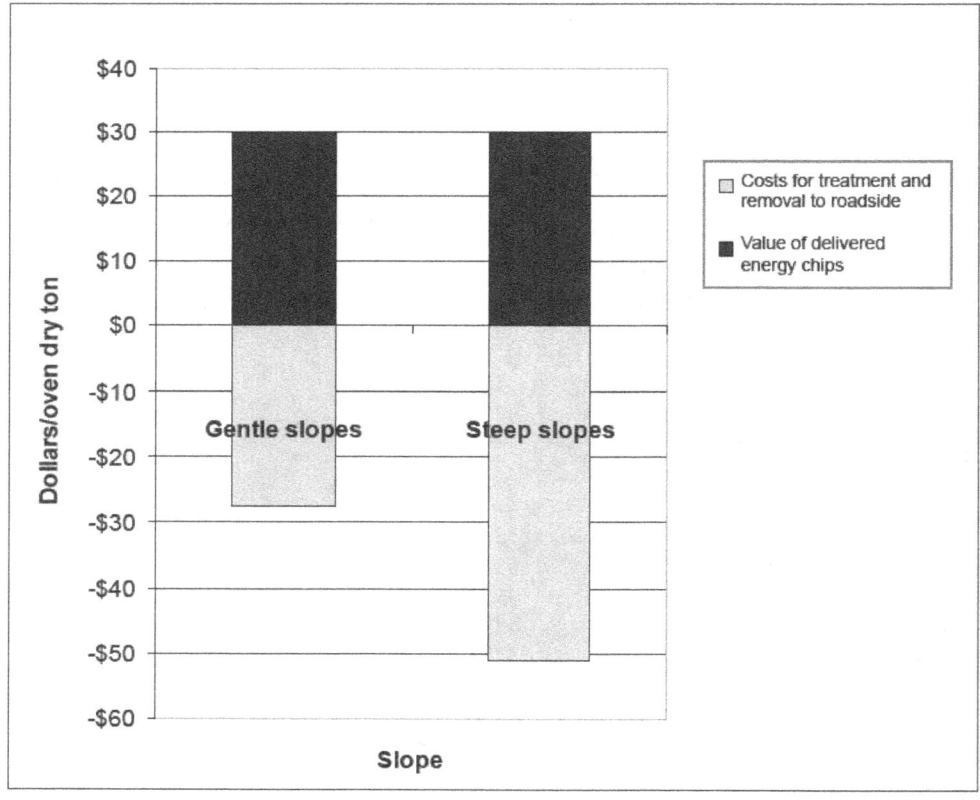

Figure 6—Simulated costs of treatment and roadside removal of hazard fuel compared to anticipated delivered values of energy chips. Data source: Adapted from Skog et al. 2006.

Table 4—Net revenue (or cost) per acre for simulated thinning regimes on public and private timberland in the Western United States

Scenario	Merchantable volume to higher value products		Chips only		Merchantable volume to higher value, plus $20 chip subsidy	
	< 40% slope	> 40% slope	< 40% slope	> 40% slope	< 40% slope	> 40% slope
	Dollars					
Uneven-age, 50% basal area removal limit, high structural diversity	533	-319	-992	-1,910	912	79
Uneven-age, high structural diversity	686	-9	-1,161	-1,917	1,159	479
Uneven-age, 50% basal area removal limit, limited structural diversity	278	-490	-971	-1,862	669	-87
Uneven-age, limited structural diversity	356	-120	-1,023	-1,909	798	114
Even-age, thin-from-below, 50% basal area removal limit	-112	-833	-973	-1,882	391	-368
Even-age, thin-from-below	-86	-762	-1,024	-1,892	441	-255
WUI, even-age, spruce-fir and lodgepole pine, 50% basal area removal limit	-144	-726	-766	-1,550	202	-478
WUI, even-age, spruce-fir and lodgepole pine, 25% basal area removal limit	-18	-266	-1,073	-1,615	421	36

WUI = wildland-urban interface.
Source: Adapted from Skog et al. 2006.

thinning regimes on gentle slopes and a limited number on steep slopes did yield a net revenue (Skog et al. 2006). In a study of hazard-fuel reduction of sawtimber material in eastern Oregon, Adams and Latta (2005) found that the form and application of the subsidy had important implications for the number of acres treated as well as the longevity of the milling capacity in local communities. A lack of milling capacity could make hazard-fuel reduction less feasible, particularly for lower valued material that is not worth transporting long distances.

Biomass Feedstock Supply Curves

Walsh et al. (2000) estimated state-level biomass supply curves that, although dated, provide a useful "data point" as one estimate of the potential biomass feedstocks available for bioenergy production at a schedule of feedstock prices. Results from a current research effort to complete county-level biomass supply curves (Dykstra et al. 2008) were unavailable for use in this report owing to the fact that portions of the research are still underway and others are restricted from distribution because of an extensive peer-review process. At the lowest delivered prices ($20/ton), residues are primarily drawn from urban waste with a small contribution of mill residues (Walsh et al. 2000) (fig. 7). In many cases, handlers of these products avoid a disposal cost by providing them to bioenergy users and thus are willing to do so at low delivered costs. At $30/ton delivered, some forest residues become available, and the supply of mill residues increases. Because most of the mill residues are currently used for other products (e.g., bark mulch), at least some of this supply will come from mill residues currently being used in other products. A small amount of agriculture residues become available at $30/ton delivered. Energy crops and the amount of agriculture residues available increase substantially as delivered prices increase. These two sources become the primary supply of biomass residue at high delivered prices. In the Walsh et al. (2000) analysis, SRWCs were not included as a bioenergy source.

Based on the estimated supply curves, the North Central and South Central regions have the greatest supplies of biomass available (Walsh et al. 2000) (figs. 8 and 9). In those regions, the majority of the supply is associated with agriculture land (energy crops plus agriculture residues). The Southeast and Northeast regions

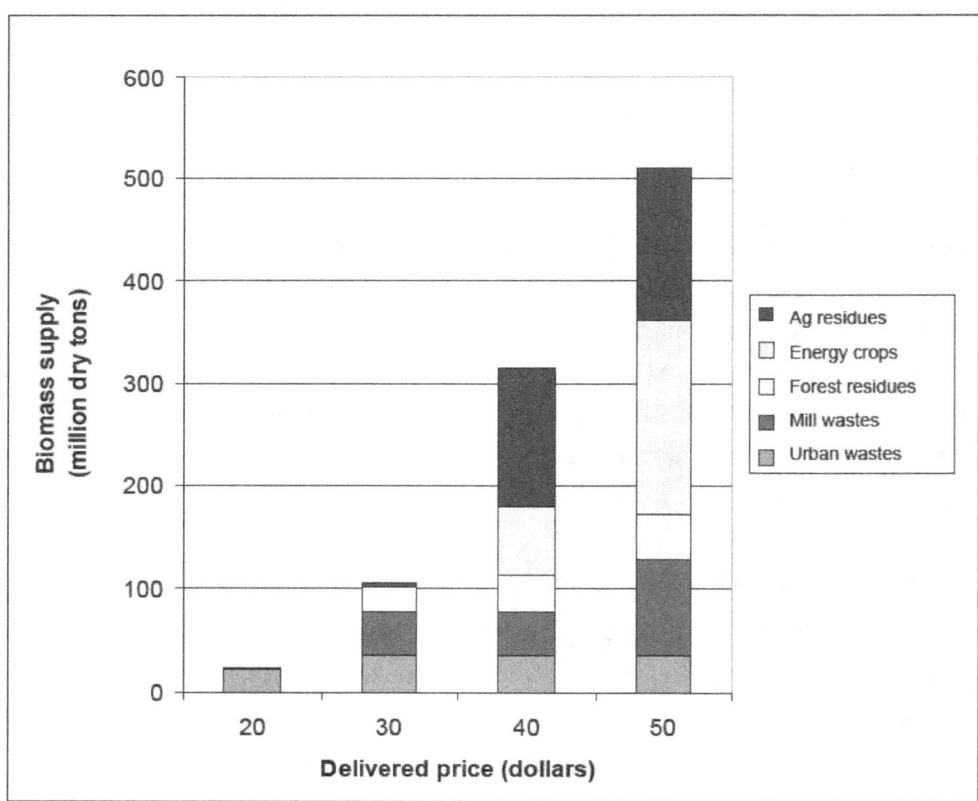

Figure 7—Estimated biomass for bioenergy supply from the contiguous United States at a range of delivered prices. Note: Short-rotation woody crops are not included. Data source: Adapted from Walsh et al. (2000).

produce a moderate amount of forest residues. As the biomass price rises to $50/ ton delivered, the supply of biomass from energy crops increases in both the North Central and Great Plains States (fig. 9). At the same time, there is a drop in crop residue from those regions, reflecting a change in planting mix to support energy crops.

Modeling Studies for Specific Biomass Resources

Short-Rotation Woody Crops

Short-rotation woody crops have been proposed as an energy crop, to provide chips for pulp and paper production, and, in the Pacific Northwest, to provide sawtimber. Current markets for products and existing yields from SRWC have not been sufficient to spur widespread SRWC planting. However, it is anticipated that climate change policies that result in a carbon price or otherwise incentivize energy generated from biomass will result in some expansion of SRWC. This expansion may come in response to SRWC being used directly to address the climate policy (e.g., energy chips to reduce carbon emissions from powerplants and tree planting to sequester carbon) or in response to changes in the forestry sector (e.g., decreased

> **Short-rotation woody crops have been proposed as an energy crop, to provide chips for pulp and paper production, and to provide sawtimber.**

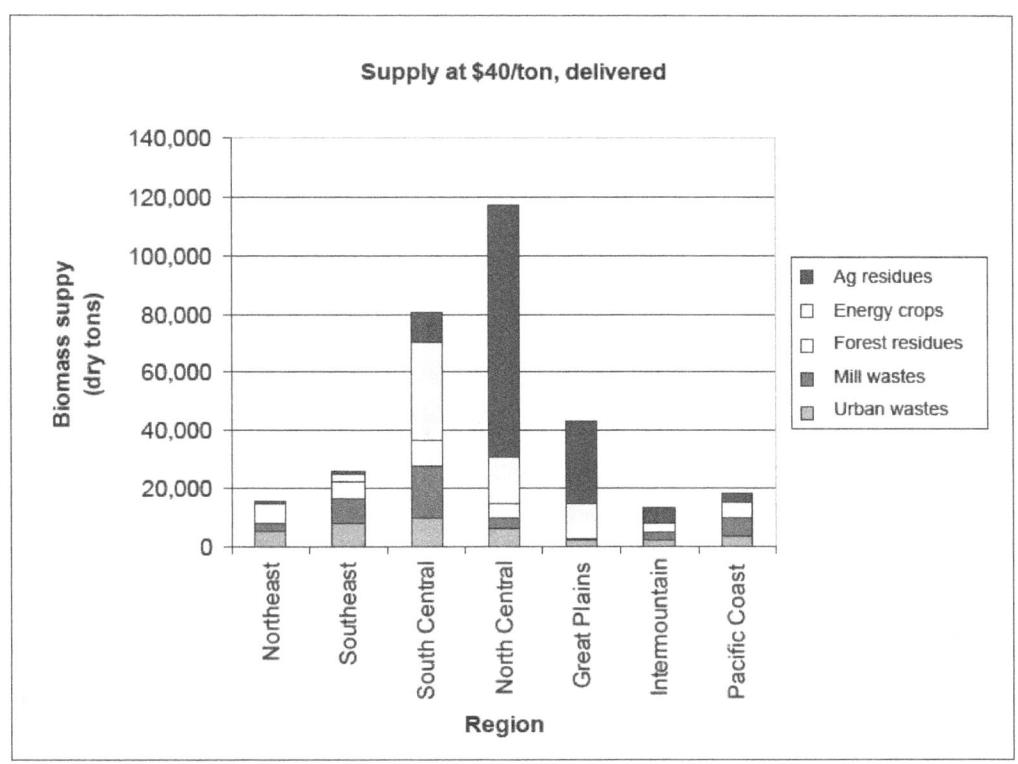

Figure 8—Estimated biomass for bioenergy by region at $40/ton delivered. Data source: Adapted from Walsh et al. (2000).

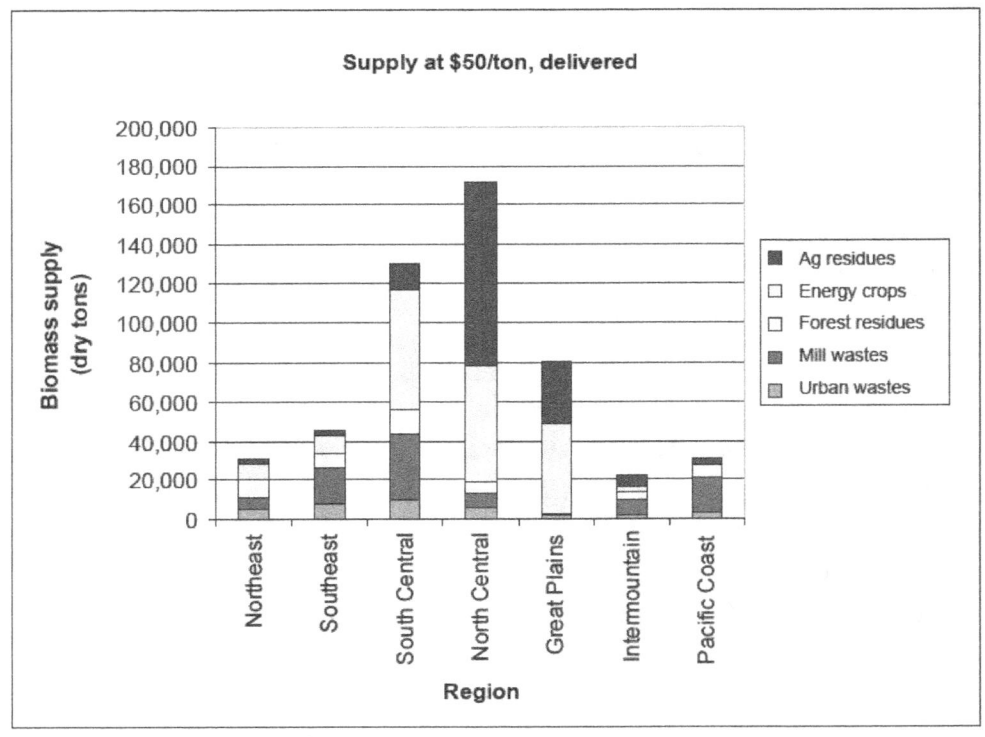

Figure 9—Estimated biomass for bioenergy by region at $50/ton delivered. Data source: Adapted from Walsh et al. (2000).

supply of pulp chips from traditional forestry sources because of increased carbon sequestration efforts).

Several studies have considered the use of SRWC for energy or pulp production. Walsh et al. (2003) considered bioenergy crop production using the POLYSYS model of the agriculture sector. The authors considered three energy crops: switchgrass, hybrid poplar, and willow. The authors assumed switchgrass could grow from the Intermountain region eastward and that hybrid poplar could be grown from approximately the Corn Belt eastward and in the Pacific Coast states. Willow was constrained to being grown in the Northern States. Two scenarios that differed in the farm price for biomass (for hybrid poplar, $32.90/dry ton and $43.87/dry ton) were considered. In the first scenario, Conservation Reserve Program (CRP) acres were treated as being managed primarily to support wildlife diversity, and in the second, CRP acres were treated as being managed primarily for bioenergy crop production. In both scenarios, landowners received only 75 percent of their CRP payment in exchange for being able to sell bioenergy crops.

In the Walsh et al. (2003) study, about 20 million acres of agriculture land were planted to bioenergy crops under the lower price scenario, and 42 million acres were planted under the high-price scenario. In both scenarios, cropland contributed more than half the acres planted to energy crops; CRP contributed most of the other acres. Hybrid poplar was planted only in the first scenario and then only on CRP lands (which were being managed with lower cost wildlife management practices). Although willow was one of the scenario options for bioenergy, it was not selected by the model. Under the first scenario, hybrid poplar plantations contributed 35.5 million dry tons of biomass for bioenergy annually. Simulated hybrid poplar bioenergy supplies were focused in the Corn Belt region, from Ohio west through Iowa, and from southern Missouri to northern Minnesota. Hybrid poplar was also planted in some areas of the Delta Region, the Pacific Northwest, and limited areas of the Northeast. The bioenergy crop choices in the results of Walsh et al. (2003) reflected the assumed comparative yields of the three crops. Model results were fairly responsive to across-the-board increases and decreases in yields. Changes in yields among the bioenergy crops were not tested.

Ince and Moiseyev (2002) extended the model reported in Walsh et al. (2003) by combining the agriculture sector model with the North American Pulp and Paper (NAPAP) model to examine the impact that hybrid poplar planted as SRWC might have on the pulp and paper sector. Although the focus of Ince and Moiseyev (2002) (and the paper discussed next—Alig et al.2000) is on SRWC production for pulp, it provides a useful reference for the amount and location of SRWC that might be planted on agriculture lands. Under current market conditions, the use of SRWC for pulp and paper production seems more likely than use in bioenergy production (Ince and Moiseyev 2002).

Under their baseline scenario, Ince and Moiseyev (2002) projected little pulp-wood production from hybrid poplar planted on agriculture lands. However, under a scenario where planting of hybrid poplar by farmers was incentivized (represented by lowering the model discount rate from 6 percent to 3 percent), the pulp production from hybrid poplar plantations increased more than threefold. The production from hybrid poplar was about 13 times the baseline in simulations where availability from the traditional pulp supply declined and the planting of hybrid poplar by farmers was incentivized. Pulp supply from traditional forestry sources could decline for a number of reasons, including forest ownership change or a change in timber management goals. In the Ince and Moiseyev model, the focus is on hybrid poplar for pulp and paper production, so most of the simulated agriculture acres planted to hybrid poplar are located in the South near existing pulp and paper manufacturing facilities. Under "high demand" scenarios, simulated hybrid poplar plantations on agriculture lands are also found in the Lake States and in the Northeast—other regions with strong pulp and paper sectors.

Both of the previous studies relied on modeling efforts built on a model of the agriculture sector. Alig et al. (2000) differed from those studies by relying on a spatial optimization model (the Forestry and Agriculture Sector Optimization Model—FASOM) that captures both the agriculture and forest sectors. One significant advantage of this approach is the ability to accommodate land transfers between forestry and agriculture as well as to capture the substitutability of product flows from agriculture and forest lands (e.g., pulp production from SRWC on agriculture lands vs. traditional pulp production from forest lands). Model results indicate hybrid poplar for pulp production would be planted on at most 2.8 million acres of agriculture land in the coming decades. The Pacific Northwest and Lake State regions showed the greatest land areas planted to hybrid poplar. Reflecting the high opportunity costs of converting cropland to another use and the lack of pulp manufacturing facilities, relatively little hybrid poplar was planted for pulp in the Corn Belt states in the Alig et al. model. The South had relatively few acres planted to hybrid poplar for pulp until the last decades of the model run. This pattern reflects the quantity of available pulp from traditional forest resources within that region.

Despite the relatively small land area devoted to hybrid poplar in the Alig et al. (2000) model, the pulp material harvested from these acres represented about 40 percent of the pulpwood material harvested in the United States in the late 1990s. The ability of high SRWC yields to offset such large volumes of pulp material could "free up" many traditional forest sector acres to be managed on longer rotations for other products (e.g., sawtimber) or for other management goals (e.g., carbon sequestration). It is possible that under a climate policy where longer forest rotations are desirable, SRWCs have the capacity to offset some of the chip material that would have otherwise gone to the pulp and paper industry.

Several implications of SRWC supply exist for the agriculture and forestry land bases. Although intensively managed, SRWCs require less cultivation, fertilizer, and other chemical treatments than many of the traditional agriculture crops and could play a key role in natural resource conservation and carbon sequestration on existing agriculture lands (e.g., Ince and Moiseyev 2002). The increased supply of hardwood pulp from SRWC lessens the demand for pulp from traditional hardwood forests, lessening the opportunity cost of converting hardwood forests to softwood plantations (Alig et al. 2000). Reflecting the linkages between the agriculture and forestry land bases, having increased pulp production from SRWC results in land transfers from forestry to agriculture (to meet crop demands) above those identified in a baseline run. This transfer from forestry to agriculture in response to SRWC production may be less significant under a climate change policy where carbon sequestration is valued.

It is possible that under a climate policy where longer forest rotations are desirable, SRWCs have the capacity to offset some of the chip material that would have otherwise gone to the pulp and paper industry.

One of the values of FASOM's combined modeling of the agriculture and forest sectors is the ability to estimate the combined welfare changes of consumers and producers in the forest and agriculture sectors. Because these two sectors are linked so strongly, examining welfare changes for only one sector could lead to inappropriate conclusions regarding welfare impacts to society from new policies or market changes. Across consumers and producers in both sectors and foreign exporters of agricultural and forestry products, the establishment of SRWC on agriculture lands (in this case for pulp production) leads to an increase in net welfare of about $6 billion. Because of a projected drop in timber prices with SRWC, forest product consumers accumulated most of the welfare gains. Those agriculture producers who planted SRWC also gain with SRWC plantations. Because timber prices are reduced in the presence of SRWC, traditional timberland owners were projected to experience a loss relative to the baseline. Because cropland values increase and short-term agriculture commodity production levels decrease when some cropland is planted to SRWC, agriculture producers, in aggregate, are projected to also suffer losses relative to the baseline case. Finally, agriculture consumers will suffer some losses because of higher prices—although these losses are relatively small. However, it is important to recall that consumers who may suffer welfare losses from consuming agriculture products are also projected to experience welfare gains from the consumption of forest sector products (e.g., paper and paperboard).

Although willow tree species did not factor into the result of either SRWC modeling efforts described above, its potential use as a bioenergy crop in the Northeast has been examined in other studies (e.g., Tharakan et al. 2005, Volk et al. 2006). Willow is often considered for bioenergy use by cofiring it with coal in Northeastern United States coal-fired powerplants. In the context of a potential carbon emissions cap under a climate change policy, cofiring willow (or any other woody biomass) with coal would yield a reduction in carbon emissions because woody biomass currently is deemed carbon neutral. Cofiring willow also reduces emissions of nitrous oxides (NO_x) and sulfur dioxide (SO_2), both of which are covered under a cap and trade program in the Northeast (Tharakan et al. 2005).

Currently, the delivered price for willow biomass is not competitive with the delivered price of coal, making widespread adoption of willow cofiring in the Northeast unlikely under the current market conditions (Volk et al. 2006). Using a systems simulation model, Tharakan et al. (2005) found that a 1 cent/kWh price premium for green energy paid by consumers or a 2.4 cent/kWh tax credit to electric producers for biomass energy would make willow production for cofiring economically feasible for electric producers, biomass aggregators, and willow producers. The modeled green price premium is consistent with "green energy" price premiums in place for electricity elsewhere in the country (Tharakan et al. 2005). An increase in willow yield of about 5 odt/ac per year, either through improved planting stock or management systems, reduced the necessary price premium 10 percent (to 0.9 cents/kWh) and the tax credit 12 percent (to 2.1 cents/kWh). The modeled yield improvement alone was not enough to make willow production economically feasible. Allowing willow to be planted on CRP lands for bioenergy production in exchange for reduced CRP payment to the landowner in a harvest year reduced the necessary price premium 25 percent (to 0.75 cents/kWh) and the tax credit 25 percent (to 1.8 cent/kWh) with current yields. Tharakan et al. (2005) did not examine the impact of a carbon price on willow feasibility. The Renewable Portfolio Standards adopted by New York and some other Northeastern States requires increased use of renewable fuels in electricity generation and may make SRWC willow plantations more feasible in the Northeast (Volk et al. 2006).

Harvest and Milling Residues

Residues from logging represent a potentially extensive source of currently unused woody biomass material for bioenergy production. However, there are technical limits to the amount of this material that can be accessed and removed, costs associated with collecting and transporting logging residues, and, in some silviculture systems, concerns about the potential impacts to soil nutrients when logging residues are removed.

In the context of firing electrical plants using woody biomass, Gan and Smith (2006) have estimated the state-level availability of residues from logging operations and other removals using 1997 FIA data. They estimated about 36 million dry tons of logging and other removal residues were available in 1997. This is consistent with the national-level supply estimated to be available at $40/dry ton delivered by Walsh et al. (2000) and that estimated by Perlack et al. (2005). Based on Gan and Smith (2006), the South Central region has the greatest amount of logging residues available, with lesser amounts available in the Northeastern, North Central, and Southeastern regions (table 5). The 36 million dry tons of logging residues were estimated to be capable of producing 67.5 TWh of electricity (Gan and Smith 2006).[3] If all of residue-generated electricity were to offset electricity generated by coal-fired plants, which is unlikely, 17.6 million tons of carbon emissions would be avoided (Gan and Smith 2006).

Extending the Gan and Smith (2006) study, Gan (2007) used 2002 state-level FIA data to estimate a national harvest residue supply curve. The estimated supply

Residues from logging represent a potentially extensive source of currently unused woody biomass material for bioenergy production.

---

[3] Gan and Smith used a conversion factor of approximately 1.9 megawatt-hours of electricity per 1 oven dry ton of wood based on a 35-percent plant efficiency.

Table 5—Harvest and other removal residues, electricity potential, and carbon emissions displaced by region, annually

Region	Recoverable residues	Electricity potential	Carbon displaced
	1,000 odt	*GWh*	*1,000 tons*
Northeast	7,551	14,088	3,577
North Central	6,982	13,026	3,694
Southeast	6,223	11,611	2,939
South Central	11,229	20,950	5,461
Great Plains	99	184	52
Intermountain	1,251	2,334	636
Pacific Northwest	1,403	2,618	716
Southwest	844	1,575	431
Total	36,197	67,532	17,621

Note: odt = oven dry ton, GWh = gigawatt hour.
Source: Adapted from Gan and Smith 2006.

curve is highly elastic for most prices. That means that small changes in feedstock price yield large changes in the amount of harvest residues supplied. For a feedstock price range of between $38 and $40/odt delivered, approximately 5 to 35 million odt of harvest residues are available, respectively. These prices assume that all the costs of whole-tree harvesting are applied to the delivered price of the biomass. If only the additional costs of collecting and transporting the biomass material is included, delivered prices decline by about $8/dry ton. A $0 stumpage price was assumed in the Gan (2007) study. The median cost for producing electricity from logging residues at an optimally sized powerplant, when only the additional costs of collecting and transporting biomass is paid by the plant, was estimated to be about $47/MWh. This estimated cost is greater than the current cost of $36/MWh for producing electricity via coal firing. The places where logging residues may be sufficient to supply bioelectricity may be limited. Gan (2007) estimates that about two-thirds of the recoverable logging residues in the United States are located in just 15 states: Alabama, Arkansas, Georgia, Louisiana, Maine, Michigan, Minnesota, Mississippi, North Carolina, Pennsylvania, Tennessee, Texas, Virginia, West Virginia, and Wisconsin.

Despite its potential supply, the inclusion of logging residues in any potential future bioenergy production portfolio is not certain. This is in large part owing to the high cost of procuring residues from the woods relative to other biomass resources and traditional fossil fuel sources. Biomass sources with very low procurement costs (e.g., mill residues) may figure more prominently than harvest residues in future bioelectricity portfolios. Using FASOM to model bioelectricity production from forest sector residue sources and SRWC, McCarl et al. (2000) found that logging residues and chips from whole-tree harvesting were not used in the production of bioelectricity; rather, in baseline projections, mill residues were relied on almost exclusively for bioelectricity plant firing. Most of the modeled bioelectricity from milling residues was generated in the South. Limited amounts of willow and switchgrass were also incorporated under baseline scenarios. When FASOM was run with SRWC yield improvements, the primary biomass feedstock was willow and some hybrid poplar in the Lake States (McCarl et al. 2000). Bark from poplar harvested for pulp was also used under high-yield SRWC scenarios. In the high-yield scenario, milling residues and switchgrass were used only when more than 650 bioelectricity plants (each 100 MW) were in operation. McCarl et al. (2000) suggested that if the goal of a government subsidy program is to avoid drastic increases in costs or to reduce emissions, a bioelectricity program that relies on milling residues in the short term and SRWC in the long term may be the most advantageous.

> **There are also a number of social, organizational, and infrastructure impediments to widespread adoption of bioenergy production.**

Challenges to Biomass Utilization

The economic challenges and some of the technical challenges to using woody biomass for energy have been highlighted in the previous sections. There are also a number of social, organizational, and infrastructure impediments to widespread adoption of bioenergy production from woody biomass, and we highlight some of those in this section. Rosch and Kaltschmitt (1999) identified five categories of challenges to bioenergy production: lack of knowledge; funding, financing, and insuring; administrative conditions; organizational difficulties; and perception and acceptance. The focus of the Rosch and Kaltschmitt paper is the European Union, but many of the points are applicable to the U.S. situation.

Lack of knowledge is pervasive across all the challenges identified by Rosch and Kaltschmitt (1999) and is not discussed separately. Many of the funding, financing, and insuring challenges have already been discussed in this paper. The existing administrative conditions, typically developed without a focus on bioenergy production, can make the permitting process confusing and cumbersome with uncertainties about the preconditions and requirements for issues unique to bioenergy production (e.g., ash disposal). Additionally, existing plant approval frameworks may not be applicable to bioenergy, resulting in confusion about the process and expectations. Administrative or legislative rules that define what qualifies as woody biomass for contribution to renewable energy targets, tax relief, or other comprehensive climate policies could impact the magnitude of future woody biomass use and the parties involved in supplying woody biomass feedstocks. The studies included here have not explored these limited eligibility issues, but researchers are beginning efforts to use the FASOM model to do so. It is difficult to examine the impacts of legislative and administrative rules on feedstock supply because many of the rules have only been proposed at this time and the definitions of qualifying material are often unclear.

In regard to organizational difficulties, numerous groups and organizations are needed for successful implementation of large biomass plants. One unique challenge is identifying an adequate network of biomass suppliers. This could be accomplished via a biomass aggregator (e.g., in Tharakan et al. 2005) or the energy producer can contract with many individual feedstock producers. The former situation is likely more attractive for the energy producer (Tharakan et al. 2005). There are also existing concerns about the lack of infrastructure for collecting, transporting, and storing biomass.

One of the greatest stumbling blocks may be public perceptions of biomass use. Rosch and Kaltschmitt (1999) remarked that there is a disconnect between the general approval of society for renewable energy production and their skepticism of generating energy from solid biomass. Rosch and Kaltschmitt highlighted three critical attitudes that are a challenge to adoption of biomass energy production. First, is the belief by some that solid biomass energy is old technology, low efficiency, and limited only to heat and steam production. This perception probably traces to past experiences with smoky, low-efficiency, residential wood stoves. Second, is the perception by individuals that energy produced from biomass is not convenient for use (e.g., inability to change heat output). Finally, many perceive that the biomass feedstock supply is difficult to obtain and may not provide a regular, reliable supply because of such things as constraints on harvest timing.

A recent case in Eugene, Oregon, may be illustrative of the productive capacity of bioenergy from biomass as well as the some of the unease regarding bioenergy production from woody biomass. In early 2009, Seneca Sawmill Company announced plans to install at a cost of $45 million an 18-MW CHP plant at their existing sawmill located outside the city of Eugene, Oregon. The expected feedstocks for the CHP plant are milling and forest harvest residues—including some residue currently sold for other products (including as pulp feedstock to a nearby mill that recently announced it will be ceasing operations). The heat produced by the CHP plant will be used for kiln drying on the mill site, and the electricity produced will be sold entirely to the power grid. The power generated would support the energy needs of about 13,000 housing units (Seneca Sawmill Company 2009). The project announcement has garnered local media attention and considerable back and forth on the local editorial page. Opponents of the plant most frequently voiced concerns about the expected pollutant emissions. Others have expressed concerns regarding the potential negative impacts to forest productivity as a result of logging residue removal and the distributional equity of where the plant (and expected emissions) are located (Eugene Register Guard 2009a, 2009b). Some opponents have stated a preference for using solar and wind energy, rather than woody biomass, to meet renewable energy portfolio requirements. In early October, 2009, Seneca Sawmill was granted an air contaminant discharge permit from the Lane Regional Air Protection Agency, allowing for construction of the CHP plant (LRAPA 2009). The CHP plant is expected to become operational by the end of 2010.

Although energy crops, e.g., switchgrass or SRWC, have great potential for use in bioenergy, the revenue to a producer from energy crops would be delayed for several years after planting while the crop matures. This results in a situation where producers are reluctant to plant energy crops because of uncertainties and delays in any potential revenues, and the consumers of energy crops (e.g., powerplants) are unwilling to invest in the infrastructure (e.g., adjustments to coal burners) necessary to utilize biomass. Volk et al. (2006) characterized the situation by stating that the large-scale deployment of willow for biomass "remains challenging because there is currently not enough willow biomass established to initiate large-scale use of the material, while at the same time there are currently no long-term commitments assuring producers of a stable market in the future." Because of this, in part, model results from FASOM (McCarl et al. 2000) indicate a short-term reliance on easily accessed feedstocks (e.g., milling residues) for bioenergy production, even though they may already be used in other products. This reliance would then shift over the long term as energy crops matured and more acres were planted to SRWC (McCarl et al. 2000).

The use of residues from forest thinning, either from hazard reduction or from other management purposes, to produce bioenergy has been extensively discussed and promoted. In addition to the economic and technical constraints discussed above, there remain a number of other challenges to the use of small-diameter thinned material from forests for bioenergy production or other products (Hjerpe et al. 2009). First, infrastructure may be limited for harvesting, transporting, and processing small-diameter material. This has resulted in part from dismantling of some harvesting infrastructure following reductions in timber harvest from federal lands. Furthermore, the remaining infrastructure capacity may not be well suited to handling small-diameter material efficiently. Second, the supply of wood may be erratic depending on market conditions and, particularly if from federal lands, harvesting policies and regulations. Finally, some individuals and organizations have concerns about hazard thinning activities that include the removal of large trees. The concern over including large stems has important implications for the effectiveness and economic feasibility of hazard-fuel thinning programs. Skog et al. (2006, 2008) have shown that hazard thinning programs that include the harvest of at least some larger stems are better able to meet targets for reducing the susceptibility of forest stands to wildfire crowning and torching. Further, those authors found that hazard-fuel reduction treatments become at least revenue neutral only if larger stems can be harvested and sold for sawtimber and pulp. On public lands, the concern over removal of large stems often manifests in an upper diameter limit on any thinning operations. Even on private lands, some individuals and groups may become concerned if they perceive that large trees are being harvested for traditional timber production under the guise of hazard mitigation or renewable energy production.

To date, many have treated bioenergy from woody biomass (and other biomass resources) as carbon neutral; biomass was treated as such under the Kyoto protocol. However, very recently some have suggested that the use of woody biomass for bioenergy may not be carbon neutral if carbon emissions from the land use change and other activities in generating the woody biomass are included in carbon emissions accounting (e.g., Searchinger et al. 2009). As an example of carbon emissions unaccounted for in biomass generation, Searchinger et al. described a scenario in which mature forest is cleared to plant energy crops. Although this example makes a useful point in fully accounting for carbon emissions in energy generation, none of the studies reported here have involved such extreme land use changes to generate biomass for energy. Much of the forest woody biomass will likely come from residues generated from harvests that would have occurred anyway or through hazard-fuel thinning operations that could reasonably be expected to increase forest growth and perhaps reduce the intensity of wildfire. The energy crop plantings included in models discussed here are primarily considered on agriculture land, much of it marginal or fallow land. In some cases (e.g., no long-term increase in crop productivity), increased energy crop planting could result in some shifts of land from forest to agriculture. Although their discussion of land use change is important, Searchinger et al. seem to ignore the land use change (e.g., mountaintop removal) that would occur under the business-as-usual use of fossil fuels relative to that land use change that might occur with biomass feedstocks. Regardless, accounting issues and carbon life-cycle emissions will be important considerations in examining policies that promote woody biomass bioenergy.

Conclusions

Bioenergy production from woody biomass is likely to be an important component in comprehensive climate change policy. Future expanded use of woody biomass in energy production will build on the current contribution of woody biomass to renewable energy. Current estimates of the potential volumes of woody biomass available for bioenergy production differ widely, primarily because of different "types" of availability that were considered and differing assumptions that were adopted in the estimates. Milling residues and wood in MSW currently have the greatest volumes of material used in production of bioenergy and other products. Logging residues currently left onsite and biomass material that could be generated as part of a hazard-fuel thinning program may offer the greatest volumes of material available and not currently used. However, handling and transport of this material is costly, and there are a number of social concerns about the use of this biomass for energy production. The acres of SRWC in production are currently very limited, but this resource may offer the most reliable and productive long-term supply of biomass for bioenergy.

The distribution of woody biomass resources is not uniform across the United States.

The distribution of woody biomass resources is not uniform across the United States. The eastern half of the United States, and the South in particular, has the greatest quantities of timber harvest and milling residues potentially available for bioenergy. Although not shown in this report, the distribution of woody material in MSW is thought to follow the population distribution, with some adjustments for recycling rates and waste generation. The West, and specifically California, has the greatest volume of material that could be available from hazard-fuel reduction. The majority of hazard-fuel reduction woody biomass is located on national forest timberland. The greatest areas of cropland suitable for production of SRWC are in the Corn Belt, Lake States, and the South Central regions. If planted for pulp production, SRWC may be most common in the South and Lake States. If planted for energy, the Northeast and possibly the Corn Belt may be the areas of planting focus.

If there is a rapid increase in the demand for biomass for bioenergy, it is likely that widely available residues (i.e., mill residues and harvest residues) will be the initial biomass feedstocks. The use of mill residues for bioenergy may reduce the supply of residue available for other products like bark mulch. As a future woody biomass bioenergy sector expands, biomass may increasingly be drawn from SRWC and thinned small-diameter material. Niche markets using woody biomass supplies unique to the local area (e.g., secondary mill residues, MSW streams) may develop in some locales.

In the United States, the current price of fossil fuel energy feedstocks and consumer prices for energy have not supported expansion of woody biomass use for bioenergy. The wood products industry, with an extensive supply of low-cost material and a large potential for reducing production costs, is the greatest producer of energy from woody biomass in the United States. In the absence of policies that make bioenergy production more attractive relative to energy derived from fossil fuels or significant changes in the price of fossil fuels, it seems that bioenergy from woody biomass will continue to remain a small component of the overall U.S. energy portfolio. However, several regions and states have implemented renewable energy standards in recent years, and bioenergy production from biomass may increase in these areas.

Additional research is needed for improved inventory and monitoring of woody biomass availability. This research should focus not only on the production volume of woody biomass (e.g., the volume generated in MSW) but also the supply that could be available at a range of feedstock prices. The lack of a reliable inventory of existing and possible supplies makes it difficult to develop an understanding of possible future outcomes. Because of recent concerns about bioenergy carbon emissions accounting, research is needed to fully consider the "additionality" and "leakage" implications for carbon emissions as a result of using woody biomass for bioenergy and comprehensive climate change policies. Research effort is also necessary to develop a better understanding of the responses in the energy, agriculture, and forest sectors to policies that would impact bioenergy usage. Few models are capable of simultaneously modeling the interactions of all three sectors. The results of previous studies using the FASOM model to examine SRWC production and increased use of biomass for bioenergy have shown the importance of examining the agriculture and forest sectors jointly. Because the forest and agriculture sectors are linked so closely, if one sector is considered in isolation, the outcomes from new climate change policies may not be properly understood.

Periodic estimates of harvest and milling residues are currently available. Estimates of the volume of woody material in MSW and at secondary wood products manufacturing facilities are generated less frequently and via a system with many assumptions about production per capita or facility. If it is desirable to use those materials for bioenergy production, more regular and rigorous efforts to quantify their volumes are necessary. More comprehensive measurements of land planted in SRWC over time will help to better identify the potential volumes that could be expected from that resource. Transportation costs are a significant deterrent to increased use of woody biomass. Better identification of the locations of current and potential bioenergy production facilities will help to identify those woody biomass resource stocks that may be in the best position for increased use. Similarly, a better understanding of the spatial patterns in supply curves for different bioenergy feedstocks (woody and otherwise) will be useful in identifying the locations where woody biomass is most likely to be used for bioenergy.

Acknowledgments

The support of Ralph Alig and the Pacific Northwest Research Station was instrumental in completing this research. The final report benefited from the helpful review comments of Darius Adams, Rob Doudrick, Dennis Dykstra, Jeremy Fried, Greg Latta, Roger Lord, Dave Nicholls, and Marcia Patton-Mallory. Thanks to Judy Mikowski for technical assistance in preparing the manuscript for publication.

Metric Equivalents

When you know:	Multiply by:	To get:
Inches (in)	2.54	Centimeters
Acres (ac)	0.405	Hectares
Miles (mi)	1.609	Kilometers
Cubic feet (ft^3)	0.0283	Cubic meters
Gallons (gal)	3.78	Liters
Pounds (lb)	454	Grams
Tons (ton)	0.907	Tonnes
Degrees Fahrenheit	0.56(F-32)	Degrees Celsius
British Thermal units (BTUs)	1,050	Joules
Tons per acre (tons/ac)	2.24	Tonnes per hectare
Cubic feet per acre (ft^3/ac)	0.07	Cubic meters per hectare

Literature Cited

Adams, D.M.; Latta, G.S. 2005. Costs and regional impacts of restoration thinning programs on the national forests in eastern Oregon. Canadian Journal of Forest Resources. 35: 1329–1330.

Adegbidi, H.G.; Volk, T.A.; White, E.H.; Abrahamson, L.P.; Briggs, R.D.; Bickelhaupt, D.H. 2001. Biomass and nutrient removal by willow clones in experimental bioenergy plantations in New York State. Biomass and Bioenergy. 20: 399–411.

AE Biofuels Inc. 2008. AE Biofuels opens integrated cellulosic ethanol demonstration plant. Focus on Catalysts. 10(10): 4.

Alig, R.J.; Adams, D.M.; McCarl, B.A.; Ince, P.J. 2000. Economic potential of short-rotation woody crops on agriculture land for pulp fiber production in the United States. Forest Products Journal. 50(5): 67–74.

Avery, T.E.; Burkhart, H.E. 1994. Forest measurements. Boston, MA: McGraw Hill. 408 p.

Bain, R.L.; Overend, R.P. 2002. Biomass for heat and power. Forest Products Journal. 52(2): 12–19.

Biomass Research and Development Board [BRDB]. 2008. Increasing feedstock production for biofuels: economic drivers, environmental implications, and the role of research. http://www.brdisolutions.com/Site%20Docs/Increasing%20 Feedstock_revised.pdf. (17 February 2010).

Carter, M.C.; Dean, T.J.; Wang, Z.; Newbold, R.A. 2006. Impacts of harvesting and postharvest treatments on soil bulk density, soil strength, and early growth of *Pinus taeda* in the Gulf Coastal Plain: a long-term soil productivity affiliated study. Canadian Journal of Forestry Research. 36: 601–614.

Dykstra, D.P.; Skog, K.; Lebow, P. 2008. Revising FRCS to update the "Billion Tons of Biomass" study. http://www.masonbruce.com/wfe/2008Program/ Dykstra_skog_lebow.pdf. (9 October 2009).

Eaton, J. 2007. Opportunities for poplar bioenergy farms in North America. International Energy Agency Bioenergy Task 30 Workshop. Portland, OR: Greenwood Resources. http://www.shortrotationcrops.org/PDFs/Eaton_Jake.pdf. (29 June 2010).

Eugene Register-Guard. 2009a. Proposed power plant raises questions about environmental costs. April 3; Sect. A:1. http://special.registerguard.com/ turin/2009/apr/3/proposed-power-plant-raises-questions-about-environmental-costs/. (17 February 2010).

Eugene Register-Guard. 2009b. Views aired on power plant. July 31; Sect. A:6. http://www.registerguard.com/csp/cms/sites/web/news/cityregion/17958982-41/ story.csp. (17 February 2010).

Farrell, A.E.; Plevin, R.J.; Turner, B.T.; Jones, A.D.; O'Hare, M.; Kammen, D.M. 2006. Ethanol can contribute to energy and environmental goals. Science. 311(27): 506–508.

FirstEnergy Corporation. 2009. FirstEnergy to repower R.E. Burger plant with biomass. Akron, OH. April 1. http://www.firstenergycorp.com/ NewsReleases/2009-04-01%20Burger%20Plant%20Biomass.pdf. (17 February 2010).

Galbe, M.; Zacchi, G. 2002. A review of the production of ethanol from softwood. Applied Microbilogical Biotechnology. 59: 618–628.

Gan, J. 2007. Supply of biomass, bioenergy, and carbon mitigation: method and application. Energy Policy. 35: 6003-6009.

Gan, J.; Smith, C.T. 2006. Availability of logging residues and potential for electricity production and carbon displacement in the USA. Biomass and Bioenergy. 30: 1011–1020.

Hjerpe, E.; Abrams, J.; Becker, D.R. 2009. Socioeconomic barriers and the role of biomass utilization in southwestern ponderosa pine restoration. Ecological Restoration. 27(2): 169–177.

Hokanson, A.E.; Rowell, R.M. 1977. Methanol from wood waste: a technical and economic study. Gen. Tech. Rep. FPL-12. Madison, WI: U.S. Department of Agriculture, Forest Service, Forest Products Laboratory. 23 p.

Ince, P.J. 2009. Scientific uncertainty about bioenergy from a forestry perspective. Greenhouse Gas Modeling Forum. http://foragforum.rti.org/documents/2.3_4_ Ince%20slides-Final%20-%20GHG%20Modeling%20-%20Shepherdstown%20 2009.ppt. (9 October 2009).

Ince, P.J.; Moiseyev, A.N. 2002. Forestry implications of agricultural short-rotation woody crops in the USA. In: Teeter, L.; Cashore, B.; Zhang, D., eds. Forest policy for private forestry: global and regional challenges. Wallingford, United Kingdom: CABI publishing: 177–188.

Johansson, D.J.A.; Azar, C. 2007. A scenario based analysis of land competition between food and bioenergy production in the U.S. Climatic Change. 82: 267–291.

Landalv, I. 2009. Pulp mills—the optimum location for biorefineries. Gasification Technologies Conference. http://www.gasification.org/Docs/ Conferences/2009/23LANDALV.pdf. (9 October 2009).

Lane Regional Air Protection Agency [LRAPA]. 2009. LRAPA issues construction permit for Seneca co-generation plant. News release October 9, Lake Regional Air Protection Agency. http://www.senecacorp.com/senecacorp/ Seneca_Permit.pdf. (17 February 2010).

Maker, T. [N.d.]. Fueling district energy and CHP with local biomass: U.S. policy considerations. Calais, VT: Energy Efficiency Associates. http://files.harc. edu/Sites/GulfcoastCHP/Publications/FuelingDistrictEnergyBiomass.pdf. (17 February 2010).

McCarl, B.A.; Adams, D.M.; Alig, R.J.; Chmelik, J.T. 2000. Competitiveness of biomass-fueled electrical power plants. Annals of Operations Research. 94: 37–55.

McKeever, D.B. 2004. Inventories of woody residues and solid wood waste in the United States, 2002. In: Proceedings of the ninth international conference on inorganic-bonded composite materials, Vancouver, BC: Moscow, ID: University of Idaho. http://www.fpl.fs.fed.us/documnts/pdf2004/fpl_2004_mckeever002. pdf. (9 October 2009).

Milbrandt, A. 2005. A geographic perspective on the current biomass resource availability in the United States. Tech. Rep. NREL/TP-560-39181. Golden, CO: National Renewable Energy Laboratory. 62 p.

Nicholls, D.; Monserud, R.A.; Dykstra, D.P. 2008. A synthesis of biomass utilization for bioenergy in the Western United States. Gen. Tech. Rep. PNW-GTR-753. Portland, OR: U.S. Department of Agriculture, Forest Service, Pacific Northwest Research Station. 48 p.

Nicholls, D.; Monserud, R.A.; Dykstra, D.P. 2009. International bioenergy synthesis—lessons learned and opportunities for the Western United States. Forest Ecology and Management. 257: 1647–1655.

Perlack, R.D.; Wright, L.L.; Turnhollow, A.F.; Graham, R.L.; Stokes, B.J.; Erbach, D.C. 2005. Biomass as feedstock for a bioenergy and bioproducts industry: the technical feasibility of a billion-ton annual supply. Oak Ridge, TN: Oak Ridge National Laboratory. 59 p.

Pimentel, D.; Hertz, M.; Glickstein, M.; Zimmerman, R.A.; Becker, K.; Evans, J.; Hussain, B.; Sarsfeld, R.; Grosfeld, A.; Seidel, T. 2002. Renewable energy: current and potential issues. BioScience. 52(12): 1111–1120.

Quesada, H.J.; Gazo, R. 2006. Mass layoffs and plant closures in the U.S. wood products and furniture manufacturing industries. Forest Products Journal. 56(10): 101–106.

Rinebolt, D.C. 1996. The potential for using wood for energy and the implications for climate change. In: Sampson, R.N.; Hair, D., eds. Forests and global change: forest management opportunities for mitigating carbon emissions. Washington, DC: American Forests: 117–130. Vol. 2.

Rooney, T. 1998. Lignocellulosic feedstock resource assessment. Tech. Rep. NREL/ TP-580-24189. Golden, CO: National Renewable Energy Laboratory. 105 p.

Rosch, C.; Kaltschmitt, M. 1999. Energy from biomass—Do non-technical barriers prevent an increased use? Biomass and Bioenergy. 16: 347–356.

Rummer, B.; Prestemon, J.; May, D.; Miles, P.; Vissage, J.; McRoberts, R.; Liknes, G.; Shepperd, W.D.; Ferguson, D.; Elliot, W.; Miller, S.; Reutebuch, S.; Barbour, R.J.; Fried, J.; Stokes, B.; Bilek, E.; Skog, K. 2005. A strategic assessment of forest biomass and fuel reduction treatments in Western States. Gen. Tech. Rep. RMRS-149. Fort Collins, CO: U.S. Department of Agriculture, Forest Service, Rocky Mountain Research Station. 17 p.

Searchinger, T.D.; Hamburg, S.P.; Melillo, J.; Chameides, W.; Havlik, P.; Kammen, D.M.; Likens, G.E.; Lubowski, R.; Obersteiner, M.; Oppenheimer, M.; Robertson, G.P.; Schlesinger, W.H.; Tilman, G.D. 2009. Fixing a critical climate accounting error. Science. 326(23): 527–528.

Seneca Sawmill Company. 2009. Seneca sustainable energy background information. Eugene, OR. http://www.senecacorp.com/senecacorp/seneca-background.pdf. (17 February 2010).

Schmidt, D. 2006. Biomass energy opportunities from hybrid poplars in Minnesota. Woody biomass harvesting and utilization workshop. http://www.extension.umn.edu/Agroforestry/biomass/schmidt.pdf. (9 October 2009).

Skog, K.E. 2007. Projecting technological change. In: Adams, D.M.; Haynes, R.W.; eds. Resource and market projections for forest policy development: twenty-five years of experience with the US RPA Timber Assessment. Dordrecht, The Netherlands: Springer: 489–511.

Skog, K.E.; Barbour, R.J.; Abt, K.L.; Bilek, E.M.; Burch, F.; Fight, R.D.; Hugget, R.J.; Miles, P.D.; Reinhardt, E.D.; Shepperd, W.D. 2006. Evaluation of silviculture treatments and biomass use for reducing fire hazard in Western States. Res. Pap. FPL-634. Madison, WI: U.S. Department of Agriculture, Forest Service, Forest Products Laboratory. 29 p.

Skog, K.E.; Ince, P.J.; Spelter, H.; Kramp, A.; Barbour, R.J. 2008. Woody biomass supply from thinnings to reduce fire hazard in the U.S. West and its potential impact on regional wood markets. In: Proceedings woody biomass utilization: challenges and opportunities. Madison, WI: Forest Products Society: 3–14.

Smith, W.B.; Miles, P.D.; Perry, C.H.; Pugh, S.A. 2009. Forest resources of the United States, 2007. Gen. Tech. Rep. WO-78. Washington, DC: U.S. Department of Agriculture, Forest Service. 336 p.

Smith, W.B.; Miles, P.D.; Vissage, J.S.; Pugh, S.A. 2003. Forest resources of the United States, 2002. Gen. Tech. Rep. NC-241. St. Paul, MN: U.S. Department of Agriculture, Forest Service, North Central Research Station. 137 p.

Stanton, B.; Eaton, J.; Johnson, J.; Rice, D.; Schuette, B.; Moser, B. 2002. Hybrid poplar in the Pacific Northwest: the effects of market-driven management. Journal of Forestry. 4(1): 28–33.

Tharakan, P.J.; Volk, T.A.; Lindsey, C.A.; Abrahamson, L.P.; White, E.H. 2005. Evaluating the impact of three incentive programs on the economics of cofiring willow biomass with coal in New York State. Energy Policy. 33: 337–347.

Tuskan, G.A. 1998. Short-rotation woody crop supply systems in the United States: What do we know and what do we need to know? Biomass and Bioenergy. 14(4): 307–315.

U.S. Department of Agriculture, Economic Research Service [USDA ERS]. 2009. Bioenergy. http://www.ers.usda.gov/features/BioEnergy/. (17 February 2010).

U.S. Department of Energy [US DOE] [N.d.]. World fuel ethanol production by country or region, 2007. http://cta.ornl.gov/bedb/biofuels/ethanol/World_Fuel_Ethanol_Production_by_Country-Region.xls. (17 February 2010).

U.S. Department of Energy [US DOE]. 2007. DOE selects six cellulosic ethanol plants for up to $385 million in federal funding. Press release February 28. http://www.energy.gov/news/archives/4827.htm. (17 February 2010).

U.S. Department of Energy [US DOE]. 2009a. Table 1.1. Energy consumption by energy source. http://www.eia.doe.gov/cneaf/solar.renewables/page/rea_data/table1_1.xls. (17 February 2010).

U.S. Department of Energy [US DOE]. 2009b. Table 8.2a. Electricity net generation: total (all sectors), selected years, 1949–2008. http://www.eia.doe.gov/aer/pdf/pages/sec8_8.pdf. (17 February 2010).

U.S. Department of Energy [US DOE]. 2009c. Table 8.2c. Electricity net generation: electric power sector by plant type, 1989–2008. In: Energy Information Administration. Annual Energy Review 2008. http://www.eia.doe.gov/aer/pdf/pages/sec8_10.pdf. (17 February 2010).

U.S. Department of Energy [US DOE]. 2009d. Table 8.2d. Electricity net generation: commercial and industrial sectors, 1989–2008. In: Energy Information Administration. Annual Energy Review 2008. http://www.eia.doe. gov/aer/pdf/pages/sec8_11.pdf. (17 February 2010).

U.S. Department of Energy [US DOE]. 2009e. Table 16. Renewable energy generating capacity and generation. http://www.eia.doe.gov/oiaf/servicerpt/ stimulus/excel/aeostimtab_16.xls. (17 February 2010).

U.S. Department of Energy [US DOE]. 2009f. Table 17. Renewable energy consumption by sector and source, scenario with ARRA investment. http://www. eia.doe.gov/oiaf/servicerpt/stimulus/excel/aeostimtab_17.xls. (17 February 2010).

U.S. Energy Information Association [US EIA] [N.d.]. Glossary. http://www.eia. doe.gov/glossary/index.html. (17 February 2010).

U.S. Energy Information Association [US EIA]. 2009a. U.S. Energy consumption by energy source. http://www.eia.doe.gov/cneaf/alternate/page/ renew_energy_consump/table1.html. (17 February 2010).

U.S. Energy Information Association [US EIA]. 2009b. Table 1.5a. Historical renewable energy consumption by energy use sector and energy source, 1989–1999. http://www.eia.doe.gov/cneaf/solar.renewables/page/rea_data/table1_5a.pdf. (17 February 2010).

U.S. Energy Information Association [US EIA]. 2009c. Table 1.5b. Historical renewable energy consumption by energy use sector and energy source, 2000–2007. In: Energy Information Administration. Renewable Energy Annual, 2007. http://www.eia.doe.gov/cneaf/solar.renewables/page/rea_data/table1_5b.pdf. (17 February 2010).

U.S. Environmental Protection Agency [US EPA]. 2008. Municipal solid waste in the United States: 2007 facts and figures. EPA530-R-08-010. Office of Solid Waste. http://www.epa.gov/waste/nonhaz/municipal/pubs/msw07-rpt.pdf. (9 October 2009).

U.S. Environmental Protection Agency [US EPA]. 2009. Estimating 2003 building-related construction and demolition materials amounts. EPA530-R-09-002. Office of Resource Conservation and Recovery. http://www. epa.gov/waste/conserve/rrr/imr/cdm/pubs/cd-meas.pdf. (9 October 2009).

Volk, T.A.; Abrahamson, L.P.; Nowak, C.A.; Smart, L.B.; Tharakan, P.J.; White, E.H. 2006. The development of short-rotation willow in the Northeastern United States for bioenergy and bioproducts, agroforestry, and phytoremediation. Biomass and Bioenergy. 30: 715–727.

Walmsley, J.D.; Jones, D.L.; Reynolds, B.; Price, M.H.; Healey, J.R. 2009. Whole tree harvesting can reduce second rotation forest productivity. Forest Ecology and Management. 257: 1104–1111.

Walsh, M.E.; De La Torre Ugarte, D.G.; Shapouri, H.; Slinsky, S.P. 2003. Bioenergy crop production in the United States. Environmental and Resource Economics. 24: 313–333.

Walsh, M.E.; Perlack, R.L.; Turhollow, A.; De La Torre Ugarte, D.G.; Becker, D.A.; Graham, R.L.; Slinsky, S.E.; Ray, D.E. 2000. Biomass feedstock availability in the United States: 1999 state level analysis. http://bioenergy.ornl. gov/resourcedata/index.html. (7 October 2009).

Westbrook, M.D., Jr.; Greene, W.D.; Izlar, R.L. 2007. Utilizing forest biomass by adding a small chipper to a tree-length southern pine harvesting operation. Southern Journal of Applied Forestry. 31(4): 165–169.

Western Governors Association [WGA]. 2006. Clean and diversified energy initiative, supply addendum. Biomass Task Force report. http://www.westgov.org/ wga/initiatives/cdeac/Biomass-supply.pdf. (17 February 2010).

Wright, L.L.; Graham, R.L.; Turhollow, A.G.; English, B.C. 1992. Growing short-rotation woody crops for energy production. In: Sampson, R.N.; Hair, D., eds. Forests and global change: opportunities for increasing forest cover. Washington, DC: American Forests: 123–156. Vol. 1.

Zalesny, R.S., Jr. 2008. Woody energy crop production. Workshop for biofuel LCIs: collection and processing. Seattle, WA: Consortium for Research on Renewable Industrial Materials, University of Washington. http://www.corrim. org/ppt/2008/CORRIM_Workshop/pdf/06_Zalesny.pdf. (28 September 2009).

Zerbe, J.I. 1991. Liquid fuels from wood—ethanol, methanol, and diesel. World Resource Review. 3(4): 406–414.

Zerbe, J.I. 2006. Thermal energy, electricity, and transportation fuels from wood. Forest Products Journal. 56(1): 6–14.